PRAISE FOR *INVITATI*

M000085238

"The drive for intimacy is real; it evolved. And this page-turner shows how a partnership can grow, indeed thrive, under extreme circumstances. It's a powerful read—vivid, humane and tragic, yet charming. Tiesel-Jensen is a savvy therapist. I got wise tips for my own partnership!"

—**Helen Fisher, Ph.D.**, *The Anatomy of Love*, TED All-Star, Match.com Senior Scientific Advisor, Senior Research Fellow, Kinsey Institute

"*Invitation to Intimacy* is luminous. It is an emotion-laden, practical, yet profound exploration of trust, intimacy, love, sexuality, and commitment, even in the face of death, from the vantage point of a devoted and ever-questioning partner in a long-term marriage (in which she and her partner just happened to be couples therapists). Within each chapter, Tiesel-Jensen seamlessly time-travels through her husband's midlife battles with Stage IV cancer, provides essential lessons via marital-therapy vignettes from their careers, and conveys impactful insights about the history of their courtship and marriage. This wondrous journey gifts readers with a marvelous sense of the potential for deeper intimacy in core relationships at any stage of their development. Top recommendation; five stars!"

—**Stephen Hinshaw, Ph.D.**, Professor of Psychology, UC Berkeley; Professor of Psychiatry and Behavioral Sciences, UC San Francisco; and award-winning author of the memoir *Another Kind of Madness: A Journey through the Stigma and Hope of Mental Illness*

"An instantly engaging, deeply appealing, honest, and highly readable look at how we conduct ourselves in our most important intimate relationships. Judy Tiesel-Jensen moves seamlessly from personal self-disclosure to professional lessons learned. The result is a memoir that reads like a novel, with a psychologist's discernment at its core."

—**Judith Warner**, *New York Times* bestselling author and *Domestic Disturbances* columnist, author of *And Then They Stopped Talking To Me: Making Sense of Middle School*

"Tiesel-Jensen effectively weaves lessons from her practice as a marriage counselor into her personal remembrance, which she conveys with thoughtfulness and delicacy. . . . [T]he author wears her professional learning lightly; this isn't an academic study weighed down by technical jargon, but a self-analysis that's written in a lucid, accessible style. An astute, forthcoming account of the heights and depths of emotional closeness."

—**Kirkus Reviews**

"This is the bravest book on marriage that you will ever read from a therapist. It's the story of the author's own marriage, with high peaks and low valleys, intermingled with the stories of her clients. You will not think of intimacy in the same way after reading this remarkable book."

—**William J. Doherty, Ph.D.**, Professor of Family Social Science, University of Minnesota, author of *Take Back Your Marriage: Sticking Together in a World That Pulls Us Apart*

"If you've ever wondered what goes on in the minds and hearts—and kitchens and bedrooms—of therapists, especially those married to each other, read Judy Tiesel-Jensen's *Invitation To Intimacy*. Even more than that, it's about people reaching within to bring out the best in themselves and how intimate relationships can facilitate that. We've been co-therapists, and she believed for our clients that intimacy heals."

—**Resmaa Menakem, LICSW**, founder of Somatic Abolitionism and author of *Rock the Boat, My Grandmother's Hands*, and *Monsters in Love*

"We don't often get a private glimpse into the intimate life of a marriage and family therapist. In this beautifully written and deeply touching memoir we are given that chance. Dr. Tiesel-Jensen takes us into the hearts, souls, and struggles of a long-term marriage and the kinds of challenges and rewards that two people face as they answer the invitation into a deepening intimacy. With a writing style that captures and compels, this book will inspire readers to garner the courage to face the personal and interpersonal challenges that will open the door to a wondrous depth of love. There are many inspiring lessons to be gleaned in this revelatory memoir and I highly recommend it."

—**Chelsea Wakefield, Ph.D., LCSW**, couples therapist and author of *The Labyrinth of Love: The Path to a Soulful Relationship*

"Dr. Tiesel-Jensen's book is an extraordinary triple threat: a wildly engaging memoir, a graduate-level course in interpersonal relationships for lay people, and an incredibly helpful text for couples' therapists. The fact that she made the book compelling reading for all three is a testament to her writing skills and her extraordinary life-experience. As one member of a long-standing intimate relationship between two mental health professionals, I can tell you that if you are interested in couples, you need to read this book!"

—**G. Richard Smith, M.D.**, Distinguished Professor Emeritus Department of Psychiatry, College of Medicine, University of Arkansas for Medical Sciences

"This book will take your breath away with its honesty, passion, spirituality, and disarming intimacy and deliver you into the heart of an amazing long-term marriage. The two lovers believed that 'relationships are life': Their journey impels us as readers to pursue deeper intimacy and provides the hope that this pursuit will open our own marriages to much more love."

—**Susan Sims Smith**, **M.Div.**, **LCSW**, Jungian psychotherapist and Episcopal priest

"Get ready for an intriguing structure that makes this book unlike any other on this topic: a very personal couples memoir intimately written with exquisite vulnerability and unprecedented honesty; a scholarly graduate marriage and family therapy teaching book; and a powerful integration of the two that brings the personal and professional together, making the complexity of couple dynamics understandable."

—**Noel Larson**, **Ph.D.**, psychologist at Meta Resources and coauthor of *Incestuous Families: An Ecological Approach to Understanding and Treatment*

"Judy Tiesel-Jensen brings the laser-pointer empathy she demonstrates in person to this memoir of marriage and loss, revealing how much she understands about how we all sometimes suffer. From a cliff-hanger opening to the final tender scenes, *Invitation to Intimacy* is a relatable book that the reader will not soon forget. It is a book for couples, for other marriage and family therapists, and for anyone who feels the urge to write her own story. Why, after all, do any of us write memoirs? To preserve those feelings? To ask the universe for forgiveness? To be remembered when no one who knew us is still alive? For all of those reasons, Judy Tiesel-Jensen has shown us that love doesn't die."

—**Elizabeth Findley Shores**, author of *Shared Secrets: The Queer World of Newbery Medalist Charles J. Finger* and other biographies

"This book has both the clarity and the inspiration to transform the lives of every couple wanting greater intimacy. There are many books on this subject, but Tiesel-Jensen's powerful story provides by far the simplest and deepest 'change tools' for close relationships."

—**Wynford Dore**, researcher and author of *Stop Struggling in School*

Invitation to Intimacy

What the marriage of two couples therapists
reveals about risk, transformation, and
the astonishing healing power of intimacy

Dr. Judy Tiesel-Jensen

Cover design and interior layout by Amy Ashford
Edited by Erin Wood
Author headshot by Meredith Melody

ISBN: 978-1-944528-26-3
Library of Congress Cataloging in Publication Data

Names: Tiesel-Jensen, Judy, 1952- author.
Title: Invitation to intimacy : what the marriage of two couples therapists reveals
  about risk, transformation, and the astonishing healing power of intimacy / [by
  Judy Tiesel-Jensen]
Description: Little Rock, Arkansas : Et Alia, [2021] | Includes bibliographical
  references. | Summary: "Reconsider the meaning and power of intimacy through
  the innermost workings of the thirty-five-year relationship between two marriage
  therapists. This candid memoir begins with a husband's dramatic diagnosis and
  weaves marital flashbacks and counseling sessions into the progression of his
  disease. Despite their degrees, licenses, and the specialized knowledge they shared
  daily with their own clients, Reuel and Judy faced the same challenges as everyone
  in lasting relationship. Through the everyday decisions and extraordinary
  movements that compose one marriage between two therapists, we see what is
  possible for every couple—the exhilarating, frightening, and ultimately healing
  power to accept invitations to intimacy in our lives"-- Provided by publisher.
Identifiers: LCCN 2021035805 | ISBN 9781944528263 (paperback)
Subjects: LCSH: Intimacy (Psychology) | Couples—Psychology. | Marriage.
Classification: LCC BF575.I5 T54 2021 | DDC 646.7/82—dc23
LC record available at https://lccn.loc.gov/2021035805

Author's Note: All clients and counseling situations are composite and
representational of actual experiences. No actual clients are represented, in order
to protect their privacy and confidentiality. Names, details, and circumstances may
have been changed to protect the privacy of those mentioned. This work represents
the author's experience and is not meant to be prescriptive or a substitute for
psychotherapy or couples therapy from a qualified professional.

Printed in the United States of America
Et Alia Press titles are available at special discounts when purchased in quantity.
For details, email hello@etaliapress.com.

Published in the United States of America by:
Et Alia Press
PO Box 7948
Little Rock, AR 72217

hello@etaliapress.com
etaliapress.com

For Aaron, Marci, and Cory:
You embody and share your father's devotion.
May your relationships continue to invite you
into the best of yourselves.

Contents

Introduction   i

Prologue   ix

1. Beginnings   1

2. Co-Constructing   8

3. Divine Presence and Dissonance   18

4. Anxiety   26

5. Truths   39

6. Trust   49

7. Doubt   61

8. Connecting   71

9. Yielding   85

10. Bonds   96

11. Christmas   101

12. Standing Firm   112

13. Letting Go   124

14. What-Ifs   133

15. Hearts   141

16. Who IS This?   152

17. Relief   165

18. Trust Again   176

19. Balancing Between   186

20. Surprises   198

21. Crossroads   206

22. Healing   220

23. "It's Enough"   232

24. Transformation   242

25. Catching My Breath   250

   Epilogue   255

   Endnotes   258

   Acknowledgments   263

   About the Author   266

Introduction

What's your favorite kind of invitation? Perhaps it's the casual, last-minute offer to go for a walk? Or the middle-of-the-week text inviting you for drinks Friday night? Maybe you prefer the formal wedding invitation that arrives in the mail, months in advance of the big day? Could it be that your favorite request involves sex?

Some invitations may be more favorably received than others, depending on our moods or comfort levels. Happy hour on Wednesday? *Of course!* Meeting your lover for a nooner? *I do believe I will!* Three-mile hike? *I just cleaned the house and washed the car, so I'm too tired.* Surprise party for a friend? *Fun, but will my ex-lover be there?* Gala fundraiser dinner-dance? *I've put on a few pounds, so what will I wear?*

When I was about ten years old, my parents and another couple were invited to the Oregon governor's mansion to have dinner with then-newly-elected Mark Hatfield and his wife. I remember my mother fretting about what to wear and which fork to use during which course, doubting she would know what to say or how to address the governor. She dreaded the possibility that she would be found lacking in some way. Fortunately, her sense of adventure and curiosity about the governor's wife was stronger than her dread, so she accepted the invitation, had a fabulous time, and talked about it for months. What if she hadn't taken the opportunity?

In contrast to formal invitations to weddings or governors' mansions and more casual but clear-cut asks, sometimes we are offered invitations that we don't even recognize for what they are. For example, when I was a college freshman and my good friend asked me out, his invitation was so subtle that I didn't realize I'd been invited—that is, until I discovered he'd been hurt by my unknowing rejection.

Intimacy requests range from the understated to the blatant, eliciting reactions of excitement, trepidation, or curiosity—even leaving us totally unaware that we've been invited. How we internally feel about and externally respond to offers can likewise run the gamut. We may decline when we really want to accept, using our calendars, fatigue, or families as excuses. Later, we may uneasily wonder why we didn't just accept or why the decision-making process was so preoccupying.

Invitations to intimacy are confusing—and by intimacy, I don't just mean sex! Intimacy is, ultimately, to know and to be known. Sex, for some, is the least intimate part of knowing or being known. As a couples therapist, I've had numerous clients throughout my years of practice who had no qualms about being sexual with someone they just met but were insulted when, after months in a committed relationship, their partner asked about their salary. Others freely share their innermost thoughts and dreams but refuse to be known physically.

The temptation to decline an invitation to intimacy is

triggered by imagining we won't know what to do or how to handle ourselves or that we'll be found inadequate to the point we would end up uncomfortable, embarrassed, or even ashamed. But if—and it's a big "but if"—we can withstand our fears about being vulnerable, our sense of adventure can emerge and take us to new heights of connecting, belonging, and attaching.

I know the truth of it. The invitation to intimacy extended to me through marriage, which I'm now extending to you through sharing my story, is exhilarating, terrifying, and soul-satisfying.

The confounding thing about intimacy is that we crave it even when we are frightened, and our fear causes us to run from it. The result is a kind of boomerang relationship to intimacy: we seek to be fully known . . . until we can't stand to be known so entirely . . . until we crave companionship.

Why do we put ourselves through such torment? That heart-throbbing, nerve-fraying kind of familiarity with another should probably send us fleeing for our sanity, except that the rewards of deep attachment keep drawing us back.

We endure and pursue because intimacy heals and transforms. The very relationships that provide healing also inflict pain and then can transform us by further healing. It can be a positive spiral, moving us in a direction of deeper and greater intimacy where we get to experience the best of ourselves. That is a profoundly powerful encounter!

This is a story about the ways that invitations to intimacy, when accepted by me and by my husband, provided healing. The invitations were rarely direct and often not identified until we were in the midst of, or had already come through, the throes of turmoil. Accepting the invitations, even when we were unaware that was what we were doing, eventually furthered our intimacy. Not the placid, plastic, feel-good-for-the-moment kind of intimacy, but the deeper kind that comes from confronting your inner demons with another, facing your pain, and offering your transparency when it feels like you may as well be naked in the Mall of America.

This is a story of my thirty-five-year marriage to a man named Reuel ("Rhoo-el"), a marriage that held so many versions of change, growth, and healing that we ultimately referred to our "four marriages" within one. In hindsight, we saw that each "marriage" arose, eventually, from our not-always-eager plunge into a deeper level of intimacy. The prickly pain of irritations about chores, the skirmishes about sex, or the slumps of depression alerted us that something needed changing. We could try to ignore an alert, or we could grow up and deal with what lay beneath it. Either way exacted a toll. Fortunately, we discovered that the cost of dealing with the problem, of facing whatever internal demons we thought we couldn't, was worth the price, because it led to emotional healing and to even greater closeness and trust.

Who knew we had so much growing up to do? There we were, two marriage therapists with four graduate degrees between us, and neither our education nor years of teaching, preaching, and helping couples could inoculate us from the pounding pressures in our own marriage. Some things we had to learn the hard way, as we all do. The lessons that were most crucial for me were ones I had to gut out as I faced my husband and, even more importantly, myself. Of course it is easier—in the short term—to avoid the demanding work of confronting ourselves or our partners. In the long term, however, avoidance does not save us from pain. And the unintended consequences of avoiding pain hamper our healing and endanger whatever intimacy may have already taken root.

The absolute wonder of those times we didn't avoid, when we each were able to confront self and other, was that they led us to encounter depths within ourselves that astonished and empowered us. We shared such sweet and tender moments that I wanted time to stop right then.

It is those experiences of accepting the invitation to intimacy—the pains and the gains—which compel me to share. We became better people, stronger people, more loving people through such full intimacy, and I believe this is possible for many couples. Through this book, I want my three children to know that; I want the maritally exhausted, discouraged, and recently singled to know that; and I want couples of all kinds—who feel they are just like us or nothing like us—who may not know they are on the verge of a radical intimacy, to recognize that it is within reach. Even those who have not been in deep relationships can find value in this story. Marriage, or coupling in any form, is not the only route to growing up. Certainly, friendships and other family relationships offer the potential for growth and healing through the practice of knowing and being known.

The crucial element for transformation of any relationship, initially, is confronting oneself. It's in the rubbing of one personality against another that we discover where our blind spots and rough edges are, where our most tender spots lie. Authentic friendships—even volatile relationships with coworkers or in-laws—offer different sets of challenges than a marriage, but can still provide contexts in which we can grow.

This memoir about wide-ranging invitations to intimacy unfolds in three parts in each chapter:

- The first part of each chapter, in italics, is a progressive narrative of our lives from the discovery of Reuel's cancer until the day he died.

- The second part in most chapters is an "Inside Look" into a counseling session or a teaching unit for Marriage & Family Therapy (MFT) graduate students. Through these snapshots, the chapter's theme is furthered by unveiling how the topic may present in the therapy office or classroom. All clients and counseling situations are a composite of the hundreds of clients I've worked with. No actual clients are represented in order to protect their privacy and confidentiality. The relational problems presented exemplify actual experiences.

- The third part of each chapter shows, through flashbacks, the intimacy struggles and victories Reuel and I experienced over the course of our lives. How, for example, in Chapter 4, our exposure to anxiety in childhood prepared us (or didn't) for the stresses and strains of marriage and what anxiety has to do with intimacy, anyway. Or how, in Chapter 8, our history of lovemaking ranged from sweet innocence to confusion, despair, and shame, but healed—at least in one instance— through accepting an invitation to deeper intimacy.

As the progressive narrative unfolds and more of our marriage is revealed through flashbacks into times of triumph and despair, I hope you will be encouraged, emboldened, and maybe even inspired. My story would be drastically different today had we not challenged ourselves and each other, through our pain, to grow and heal together. We pushed each other to meet the demands of intimacy, not always knowing what the payoff would be. The rewards, it turned out, included a nourishing devotion to each other, passionate sex, a contentment in each other's presence, and a grateful joy to be mates in body, mind, and spirit.

What we couldn't have anticipated through our struggles and rewards, nor hardly bear to consider, was that our marriage would end prematurely. The unforeseen gift of giving intimacy was that it sustained and strengthened us and our children through the death of my husband and our marriage and into a new life beyond.

I invite you, dear reader, to know me and Reuel. By sharing our adventures in intimacy, I hope you'll be stirred to experience or deepen intimacy in your own life and relationships.

Prologue

I ended the phone conversation with my gynecologist, then doubled over to keep from throwing up. I couldn't find enough oxygen in my lungs to tell my husband what I'd just heard: I had an STD, a sexually transmitted disease. Questions pinged like pinballs through my mind, lighting up my nerves, but they all dropped into the same hole: *How could this happen?* I sat up suddenly and looked at Reuel like he was a foreign creature. We'd been married for thirty years, but did I really know him? I knew he'd been frustrated with our sex life off and on over the course of our marriage. *Has he had an affair?* My gut twisted. I hadn't cheated, so the STD must have been transmitted through him. My mind raced backwards to review everything I knew about him, about myself, and about our marriage. I thought I knew us. *What could have happened?*

1
Beginnings

Fourth Week of May

My 8 a.m. appointment has just finished, and I'm about to bring in my next client when Reuel calls on my private line. He's at the hospital just down the street, having an MRI before receiving a routine spinal injection to relieve some of his back pain. His voice is low and urgent.

"I need you to come over here right away. They found something in the MRI."

I'm suddenly dizzy. I cancel my next three appointments and head out the door only to see my 9 a.m. client—one half of the couple—still in the waiting room.

"So sorry, but there's been an emergency, and I'm on the way to the hospital," I explain. I see his look of alarm and try to reassure him. "No, it's not his heart." He looks relieved, and I try to take some relief for myself.

I slow my breathing as I park in the emergency parking lot and dash to the first desk after the entrance. The red-coated volunteers immediately show me to the same-day surgery unit. My legs wobble when I pass the nurses' station, and I wonder if they are looking at me like they know something.

I turn into a private room and rush to hug Reuel. He is as white as the surroundings. He begins to explain what the doctor told him when the doctor himself appears with the MRI films. The doctor's color isn't good, either—has our whole world been drained of life?

"This was just a routine X-ray prior to his injection," the doctor explains as he puts the films on the light box. "See this area right here? This is his upper spine."

"Yes," I respond automatically, although I don't really know what I'm seeing.

"These white blotches . . . here, here . . . and here?"

"Yes . . . " I glance at Reuel, who is looking down.

"These spots are tumors."

"Oh!" My breath catches, trying to think what this means. "Well . . . what kind of tumors?"

"Unfortunately, they're malignant." He turns to me and doesn't break eye contact. "And this is not the primary site of the cancer. It has metastasized to his spine." Before I have a chance to ask, he answers. "We don't know where it started, just that it has spread here."

"Is this what was causing his back pain?" I ask, trying not to voice my accusation about how the doctor could have missed this.

"No, the tumors are not in the right spot for that." He shakes his head. "I'm just so shocked at this."

You're shocked? My insides have turned cold.

Reuel's eyes seek mine, and we lock onto each other to will ourselves strength and will away the foreign invader.

 Inside Look: Downtown Minneapolis Counseling Clinic, Early Career

"One of the things I like to ask couples," I say to the new clients in my new-to-me office, trying to sound more experienced than I am, "is what first attracted you to each other?" The angry, middle-aged spouses sitting across from me suddenly soften. They shoot a glance at each other, a hint of a smile around the husband's mouth. I can tell he will need to be the first one to share since the wife looks hesitant. Their eyes are distant from recall but warm as they transport themselves to a happier time.

Over the years, when I've asked about that first attraction or first meeting, some couples have described the electrical charge they experienced. A few called it "love at first sight," and some have expressed it as an instant intimacy.

That definitely was *not* my experience upon meeting Reuel.

The first time Reuel and I were asked about our attraction to each other was two years into our marriage. We were in the middle of a marriage enrichment weekend and had survived all the forced intimacy pretty well when we got to the "Attraction Exercise." I glanced around the big room at the other couples paired off, chairs facing each other, when I began to squirm in my own chair, clueless about the source of my discomfort. I locked eyes with Reuel. He smiled and started first.

"I thought you were gorgeous, with your body and your long, blonde hair. And you had this quiet strength of knowing who you were." *Really?* I just looked at him, stunned.

It took a while for me to respond, my discomfort building. "I first fell in love with your voice. The way you hit those high notes when you sang 'Bridge Over Troubled Water'? Melted me! But what really clinched it was how you looked at me and listened to me . . ." I swallowed and looked down. "To be honest, though, I wasn't initially attracted to you."

"Okay, I'm not sure I've heard about this, but tell me! I want to know."

Ugh. This was supposed to be marriage enriching? "Well, do you remember when we first met? I was fifteen and not as sure about who I was as you thought. Really, though, I should tell you about three different times when the way you looked at me began to work its way into my heart." That heart of mine began to beat double time as I spoke, and I couldn't hold eye contact. It didn't occur to me that I'd ever have to reveal what I originally thought of him. *Will it hurt him, squash his ego?* I wondered to myself.

"Let me just tell you before I chicken out," I said as I gathered my memories.

"That first time, when I was fifteen, I was with the group heading back home to Walla Walla from a youth convention in Minneapolis. Since your parents knew some members of our group, they had invited us to stop at your house for lunch. My friend, never-shy Sally, invited herself and me to ride along with your dad to pick you up from work so you could join us.

"'There he is,' Sally whispered, when she spotted you across the parking lot.

"And there you were: tall and lanky, with a gap between your front teeth and your faded-cotton, paisley shirt that looked two sizes too small. All topped by your thick

4

shock of dark, wavy hair. *Yeah, he looks like an MK,* I thought, our slang for a 'Missionary Kid.' But then, when your father introduced us, your sparkling brown eyes riveted me, like you knew something I didn't."

I braved a glance at Reuel. He waggled his eyebrows.

"The second time was the summer before I left for college. I was so desperately bored in that wheat town, itching for a distraction, and then I saw your college quartet was scheduled to give a concert at our church. Do you remember that night?"

He nodded.

"You did not look like an MK nerd that night! More like tall, dark, and . . . okay . . . handsome. When the pianist started the introduction to 'Bridge Over Troubled Water,' you looked right at me before you started the solo. Again, it was like you knew something. I still remember my cheeks got red, then I got goosebumps when I heard you sing. After the concert, you asked me lots of questions, and you really looked at me when I talked."

I paused to catch my breath. *So far, so good,* I thought, but having to describe the next contact made me the most uneasy.

"The third time was when I arrived at college. My parents and little brother helped move me into the dorm, then unpacked my electric corn popper—remember all the popcorn I made?"

"Yeah . . ." Reuel seemed to be encouraging me to get to the point.

"Well, I finally got the family out to the grassy hill, closer to their car, but then another set of parents joined us, and I thought they'd never leave. Just then, you came loping down the hill and spotted me. Remember what you said?"

"Uh, 'Welcome to campus?'"

"Yes, and again you looked straight into me. I remember thanking you but quickly breaking eye contact and introducing you to the others. Then, you looked at me and asked what I was planning to do next."

"Hoo, I remember now!" Reuel interrupted. "You were kind of squirming and wouldn't look at me."

"Yeah, I wasn't sure you were cool enough for my plans for popularity, even though you were the best singer on campus, and I didn't want you to think we were going to be very good friends. You told me to have fun getting settled, but some of the smile left your voice. Then, you jogged down to the campus center.

"My mom's eyes followed you down the hill, and she demanded, 'Judy, who was that?'"

"'Oh, that's Reuel Tiesel,' I told her, 'and I can't stand him.'"

There it was. I had told him I wasn't initially attracted to him. I held my breath, waiting for Reuel's reaction. His head was down. Was he crushed? Angry?

"Hah!" He burst into laughter with a twinkle in his eyes and wagged his eyebrows again. "Lucky for you, my voice and eyes are irresistible!"

Years later, at our thirtieth wedding anniversary party, and again at the intimate gathering the night before his funeral, my mother described that encounter on the hillside with both glee and reverence. "I knew," she told our friends, "that was not the last I would see of Reuel Tiesel. I had a feeling go through me that he was going to be an important part of our lives." My mom, the queen of understatement.

Co-Constructing

"Intimacy isn't something you have. It's something you do."
—Terry Real

Fourth Week of May to Third Week of June

The doc who just explained that our world is about to fall apart sends us back to Reuel's family physician, whom he says will "quarterback" the series of tests now needing to be done. We step to the front desk of our clinic, notorious for its lengthy waits, to announce our arrival. A nurse appears out of a nearby room and immediately takes us back to a private area where the doctor will see us. I'm trying to decide whether these familiar faces from our family clinic look shaken, or maybe I'm shaken and projecting. Then Reuel's long-time doctor enters.

"What happened?" the doctor asks, shaking his head as he reads the radiology report.

"No, that's my question," returns Reuel. "I'm supposed to be the one with the questions, Doc. How did this happen? And what is *happening?"*

"That's what we're going to find out," he begins, now very businesslike, and launches into a litany of diagnostic procedures to be

scheduled. I'm taking notes like crazy, tracking which test needs to be done in what order and trying to detect what they suspect is the original site of the cancer. My note-taking keeps my mind from falling into a hole I might not be able to climb out of.

The doctor's voice softens. "But most importantly, how are you doing?"

This sudden switch from business to empathy catches me off guard and does the same for Reuel, judging by the tears splashing onto his cheeks. There's nothing we can say.

"We will do everything we can," he assures us, "and here are two phone numbers, the direct number to my nurse and the number of the oncologist I'm referring you to. All the test results will also go to him so he can plan treatment."

We now have an oncologist. Does anyone ever want an oncologist? That must rank up there in least desired acquaintances, right next to those in my dad's profession of funeral director/embalmer.

The next two weeks are spent setting appointments, juggling work schedules, and letting friends and family who are scattered around the country know this news. Aaron, our oldest child, is plying his pastry-chef training on a cruise ship based in Hawaii, an experience he refers to as "indentured baker-tude." Marci, who boldly plays the middle-child-and-only-daughter status whenever it is to her advantage, is waiting tables at an upscale restaurant in the Mall of America until she gets her photography career off the ground. Cory, the youngest, has been living in New York City ever since he went to acting school there. He is also waiting tables to pay bills. They react to their dad's diagnosis in characteristic ways: Aaron sounds matter-of-fact, Marci wells with tears, and Cory shifts from fearful concern to anger.

Reuel, meanwhile, is fasting or flushing as the tests require. The results rule out some primary cancer sites, but nothing is definitive by the time we go to the first oncology appointment. We take the stairs to the second floor, grateful at least for that strength.

The waiting room is crowded. Every table holds baskets of hard candies. Ah, to help quell the nausea from chemotherapy, I realize. We step to the receptionist's desk. She can't find Reuel's name anywhere. He has already sent the preliminary paperwork, but she can't put her hands on it. He repeats his name and date of birth two more times as she shuffles files. Maybe this whole thing has been a mistake, a complete misunderstanding, a nightmare from which we are about to wake up.

Not yet. Reuel decides to lighten the tone by cracking a joke about the candy. The receptionist is not amused, which throws us into fits of suppressed giggles. We sit and wait and watch the patients be called back: young, elderly, strong-looking, frail-looking, some with hats or scarves, some with full heads of hair. I look to see who goes for the candy but can't detect a pattern.

Finally, a male nurse calls us back and verifies the information Reuel has given them.

"Allergies?" the nurse asks.

"Well, Compazine gives me a psychotic reaction. Too many people in my head having conversations with that medication." Reuel looks at me and smiles as we remember the time he took it for nausea control but reacted by hearing voices.

"Then how are we going to control your nausea from the chemo?" the nurse shoots back.

We are stunned into silence. The nurse is oblivious to our reaction and finishes up his questions. He assures us the doctor will be right in and leaves the room.

Simultaneously, we erupt with raw reactions.

"How does he know you're going to even need chemo?" I ask, outraged.

"That's pretty stark to say to us when we don't yet have a diagnosis. We need a little of our denial still intact."

We wait. The oncologist knocks and enters. Slight of build with dark features, he introduces himself to each of us and makes the right amount of chit-chat. Then he looks at the chart, and we go silent. Is Reuel holding his breath like I am? Are we going to be bound to this mild-mannered, dapper specialist for the foreseeable future? Do I like him? Yeah, I do, *I think as I listen to him and watch his nonverbal responses to Reuel.*

Then he clears his throat, the equivalent of a drum roll.

"We have determined the source of the tumors on your spine. It is non-Hodgkin's lymphoma, and unfortunately, it is Stage IV."

He pauses, watching our reactions. I suddenly feel like I'm up in the corner of the ceiling, watching this scene play out below. Reuel begins with questions.

"What does Stage IV mean, and how serious is it?"

"Stage IV means the cancer has spread beyond the original site. That is quite serious. But we have some very effective chemotherapy treatments to combat it, and you have several points in your favor to fight this cancer. After all, you are basically a healthy young man. Have you seen the average age in my waiting room? Your preliminary tests show you have a sound heart and liver."

I think, Basically healthy, *you mean, other than the Stage IV lymphoma? He offers more information about non-Hodgkin's lymphoma, that it originates in the lymphatic system, and something about the size of the cells and the need to start chemo immediately. I should be taking notes, I suddenly realize, but my hand and brain aren't communicating. About the time Reuel asks how long until his hair falls out, my pen finally starts moving on the paper. "3 weeks after first Tx," I write. "1 Tx every 3 wks x 8 Tx's."*

That's six months. Holy shit!

We set a date for the first chemotherapy treatment and sign up for classes to learn how to be good patients and caregivers. The patient brochure informs us, in case we somehow missed it, that "cancer impacts the whole family."

 ### Inside Look: Counseling Office in West Central Minnesota, Reuel's Early Career

I'm here to pick Reuel up from his weekly volunteer counseling, and he is totally charged. "Judy, I used a word today with this couple, and it so fit everything I believe about relationships. It really helped me explain what was happening in their marriage." He is packing his notes into the file cabinet.

"C'mon, what is it?"

"Co-constructed. I think I just made it up. I was searching for a term to describe how they—or any couple—agree to handle things a certain way, whether they fully realize it or not. Like this couple I just saw: he has been drinking too much, so she starts to count the bottles in the trash, then she looks for his hiding places around the house, but she never talks to him directly about how much and how often he is drinking. Gradually, she takes over control by buying his liquor and rationing a bottle to him every so often. She has taken responsibility for his drinking, classic enabling!"

"Okay, but I'm not sure about how that fits with 'co-construction.'"

"Well, they have co-constructed how they handle his drinking in their marriage. Of all the options available to deal with it, they have settled into this pattern. They've implicitly agreed, or co-constructed an agreement, that he drinks, and she manages it. That is what has become normal for them."

We didn't always know we were co-constructing our relationship, especially in the early years. The first time Reuel came to visit me at my home, for example, tested his flexibility. It hadn't occurred to me to warn him that my father owned a funeral home where our family lived upstairs. When we pulled up to the mortuary for the weekend stay, he looked at me and smiled. "Nice one. Now where do you really live?"

"Uh, this is where I live. I thought you knew."

"I'm going to stay in there tonight? You're really not kidding?"

I should have known it was true love from what he was willing to endure for me that weekend: a chronic state of jumpiness, peeking around every corner, flinching at unfamiliar sounds, and bounding down the stairs to escape at every opportunity. Inadvertently, we were establishing some patterns of courage and flexibility, with a good dose of humor.

One night, after we had been dating for several months, Reuel was at my house. He said goodbye to my family and was heading down the back stairs when I heard him talking.

"Who are you talking to? " I called down to him.

"Oh, I always say, 'Goodnight, Fred,' 'Goodnight Myrtle' to whatever guests in caskets you have down here. It's less creepy that way." I looked at my mom, and we tried not to giggle.

Later, his parents and roommate asked how he could do it, always going in and out of the funeral home. Doesn't it gross you out? How can you stand it? As an indication of his flexibility and humor, he responded with a line he took from my grandpa: "It's not the dead ones I worry about . . ."

Looking back, I recognize now how an event one year into our marriage set some co-construction patterns about how we would operate when Reuel was worried or we were fighting.

We had plenty to figure out that first year of marriage: moving to the Midwest, finding a job to support Reuel through seminary, and sorting out cooking/cleaning chores. By the end of that first year, I also realized I lived in a tired, worn, factory town, and I was lonely. Fortunately, that was just about the time my good friend from high school, Janet, transferred to the same college that housed the seminary, and I finally had a friend to do things with. We wasted no time coordinating our work schedules in order to plan a day out together: drive to Indianapolis, shop, see a movie, talk, and have fun. Reuel was not nearly as excited as me, but he tried to be a good sport about it since he knew of my loneliness. Once our plans were made, my whole body felt lighter with anticipation.

Finally, Janet and I headed out early on a Saturday afternoon, happy and free, singing along to the radio. We caught up on news from home, compared reports from our families, and dished about her latest love interest. The trip of forty-five miles to Indianapolis flew by, and after some shopping, we decided to go to the trendy new movie, *The Way We Were*. We dashed to make the next showing, and by the time it finished, we were famished. During dinner and through the drive home, we discussed the movie, caught up in the poignancy of the love between Redford's and Streisand's characters.

"Do you really think he was trying to change her?" I wondered aloud.

"Yes! She needed to be her own person. And so did he."

"But they loved each other! And then they gave it all up. I don't get it . . ." I pondered, a little troubled.

Even so, I was delighted from this day spent with my friend, recapturing what it was like to be purely me, Judy the friend, free of the descriptors of "new wife" and "new in town." As we turned into our driveway, I saw movement by the front window right before the front door swung open. Reuel stepped out on the front step, and I could see despite the darkness that he was fuming. Janet and I looked at each other and both breathed an "uh-oh." I said goodbye, and my perfect day slammed to a halt.

I walked up to kiss Reuel hello, but instead he cried out, "Where have you been?"

"Uh, with Janet. On our day out." I didn't understand his reaction.

"I have been worried sick! I never dreamed you would be out this late. I was just about to call the State Police."

"What?" I was stunned. "Really?" He was clearly over-reacting, but I knew enough not to say so.

"Did it ever occur to you to call me and let me know

you'd be late?"

Well, no. No, it hadn't. I didn't know I was "late." I didn't know I had a curfew. My head swam, but whether it was from Reuel's (over)reaction, or from the emotional whiplash between his response and the movie Janet and I had just been discussing, or from my own reluctance to acknowledge any responsibility, I didn't know. I was confused. I had not seen Reuel like this, and I was alarmed.

"I had visions of you smashed in a car wreck, or assaulted in a parking lot, or . . ." he faltered, voice cracking. "I've been so worried I haven't been able to do homework, sleep, or anything."

His fear was now more understandable to me. "I'm really sorry you've been so worried. I had no idea it would be so upsetting to you, and I didn't want that to happen."

He looked at me. "Do you think it's unreasonable to ask that you call to let me know what's happening?"

I waited a few beats. "No, I think that's fair. I'm sorry I didn't call."

My insides were unsettled as if I had vertigo, which I would come to learn was a physical clue that something was off-balance, like an uncentered load in the washing machine. I sorted through my thoughts: I loved my new husband, and I loved being loved, but what about my need to have my own friends? What if he didn't like my need? Nope, I was not going there. It was a harder conversation.

It didn't occur to me to ask Reuel about how quickly his mind jumped to catastrophes, how ramped up his body was with worry. I was new to this state of marriage, so figured I must be in the wrong since I clearly did not consider my spouse and created so much stress for him. I felt sorry he was in so much pain, but I also felt angry. Something in this scenario didn't seem fair. How would Streisand's character in the movie have reacted? She would have told Redford's character to back off, to quit trying to control her. And eventually she would have backed him off to the point of losing him. I didn't want that, didn't want to lose Reuel. I could see that it was reasonable for me to call him when I was going to be late. I did not yet grasp what was reasonable for him, what his part was in this equation of co-construction.

It would be even longer before I understood the imperative to confront him with his part. Or to trust myself and him enough to know I didn't have to forego a powerful love in order to be fully myself. What we were co-constructing then, I would realize later, would have to undergo deconstruction and remodeling in order to clear enough space for intimacy.

3
Divine Presence and Dissonance

"The road to enlightenment is long and difficult,
and you should try not to forget snacks and magazines."
—Anne Lamott

Second and Third Weeks of July
Reuel's first chemotherapy treatment is now just a week away. After going to the chemo classes and hearing the range of patient stories and potential side effects, I decide it's a good idea to purchase a recliner for the first time. Reuel is feeling fine physically, but he's already lost ten pounds from the stress. "A helluva way to diet," he says to his coworkers, a team of eight mental health therapists. Still, I can't imagine how this strong, fifty-six-year-old man is going to tuck his 6'4" frame into a recliner.

It's Sunday morning, the day before chemo starts, and we relax with coffee, the newspaper, and our favorite classical music program. The sun gleams through the wall of windows and for a moment we watch the wetlands area that spreads all along the back of our property. The pond is alive with thrusting fishing birds and bob-

bing goslings. We glance at each other every once in a while, smile, and go back to reading. *Is he wondering the same thing I am? Is this our last and best Sunday for a while? How will our sacred Sunday mornings change?*

I remember that the recliner is to be delivered this morning just as the doorbell rings. I open the door to admit our new chair and am surprised that the delivery man backs away. He points up to the roof.

"Hey, did you know there's a bald eagle circling your house?"

We run out front, spot it, and dash to the back of the house when the eagle changes course. We see it pause, almost as if it's confirming its presence to us before it soars upward and away. I look at Reuel, who is still searching the sky. Tears are streaming down his face. I'm moved by the eagle too, but his intense reaction puzzles me.

I direct the delivery man to the correct corner of the room for set-up. He continues to rave about seeing a bald eagle so close while he returns to his truck to leave. I thank him, close the door, and turn to ask Reuel about his tears.

"A few weeks ago," he says, "I was talking with the Divine and wondered if it might be okay to ask for a sign of the Divine's presence during this journey. The Divine asked me what I would like, so I thought a while—you know what I'm like when I have to ask for something. Finally, I decided to ask for an eagle." His voice was quiet and awed. "I had forgotten about it until the delivery guy said there's an eagle circling our house."

Now I'm crying also. We hug. We feel less alone with a Divine presence to begin chemotherapy. It's gonna be okay.

 ## Inside Look: Pastoral Counselor's Office, Southern Virginia, Pre-Career

"Ok, Judy, I hear you were embarrassed by Reuel's actions in front of the congregation. Yes, I realize it is his first congregation, and the leaders at church headquarters are watching him. But I want to tell you something important. If Reuel wants to make an ass of himself, he can do it. It doesn't mean that's about you or reflects on you. His being an ass, if that's what he was, is squarely on his . . . well, ass. The two of you may have very different ideas about how things should be done in the church. In fact, you may have very different ideas about God. Is that okay?"

God and intimacy. That pairing may either confirm your understanding or creep you out. We each bring our unique experiences to whether God and intimacy should be in the same sentence, which is, in part, why God and intimacy can be a big deal in any marriage. Even among friends, when conversations veer toward the subject of spirituality, a Higher Power, or religion, tensions can surge because we get so invested in our personal sense of meaning that we want others to see it the same way. The God of our understanding reflects an ultimate value, a way of seeing the world and creating meaning. A couple's approach to this sense of an "Ultimate" or Higher Power in their lives has the potential to lead to great joy, but also great conflict and, sometimes, tremendous pain. It's an area where, unfortunately, all the unresolved power and control issues can gather, turning spouses into religious bullies. I've seen it happen at every spot on the religious continuum, from liberals bullying their queer partners to conservative husbands bullying their "non-submissive" wives to religious professionals pulling their "clergy card" in an ultimate power play.

How does a couple navigate such religious or Ultimate terrain?

Sometimes it's a non-issue for a couple, such as when one couple agrees that they don't care about religion, or another couple agrees to organize their lives around the church, mosque, or synagogue. Conflict comes when one of them changes the agreement, the understanding they've co-constructed, and the other doesn't like the effects of the change.

Reuel and I started our marriage in agreement about the role of God and ministry in our lives, but we changed. It wasn't a dramatic change. In fact, in the beginning, the changes were so subtle that it was hardly worth noticing. Over time, however, the impact of the changes picked up momentum until we could not ignore it. Embedded within the changes was an assortment of invitations to intimacy.

I knew from the time I was little that I wanted to marry a minister. Of course, if I were growing up now, I would just become a minister myself, but in my late-1950s childhood, the most efficient route of fulfilling my dream was to marry one. I tucked away my private certainty about marrying a minister until one night after Reuel and I had been dating for several months. We had deliberately not talked about our future together or the "M" word. He was walking me back to the dorm when he said he needed to tell me about his new direction.

"I've come to believe over these past several days that God is calling me to ministry. I don't know if it means the pastorate, but I know it's ministry of some kind," he said. Then he stopped and stared at me. "What's wrong?" He looked taken aback.

I was gaping at him like he'd just invented chocolate. "Oh." I fidgeted a bit, then just blurted out, "I always thought I would marry a minister!"

Reuel's eyes grew wide. He opened and shut his mouth a few times. "I have to go study," he said and fled to his dorm.

Ultimately, we did marry and move to that Indiana factory town for Reuel to attend seminary. Following graduation, he pastored for eighteen years across five different congregations in four states, experiencing the best and worst of congregations. At their worst, congregation members can inflict great pain. Personally, our experiences included members going through our garbage to start rumors, bullying at board meetings, and organizing deliberate deceptions to neutralize the pastor's influence so leaders could keep secret their sexual inappropriateness among the members.

Many clergy couples turn away from each other in their pain, but it drew us closer. We knew we needed support, though, so we made a practice of seeing pastoral counselors when the stress grew unmanageable. The last congregation he had served was a particularly poisonous system, and Reuel's body seemed to absorb the toxins from the community, like a "sin eater." After he resigned, it took some time for his body and spirit to recover, but when it did, he was thrilled to move into a new career as a full-time counselor.

And I was thrilled to see him so happy about this new direction in his life. Imperceptible to us at the time, our religious "tracks" that had been running parallel for all these years gradually began to shift, so that the tracks grew further apart the farther down the marital road we got.

The first time Reuel used the word "Divine" in our conversation instead of "God," my eyebrows raised. *That's odd,* I thought. This was during the time he had been doing intense healing of childhood trauma, and I had begun to see changes in him. Over the next few days, he spoke of "the Divine" several times, and each time he said it, I got increasingly irked. Finally, one Saturday, I could no longer contain my irritation.

"Why are you saying that?" I demanded, sorting dirty clothes into piles.

"Huh?" he paused as he picked up the laundry basket.

"Using the word 'Divine.' Why aren't you saying 'God?'"

"Well, as I've been —"

"It sounds so pretentious. What's wrong with 'God?'"

"Well, what I —"

"Are you rejecting everything you've known and loved?" I was surprised by my own question.

Reuel set the laundry basket back on the floor. "What are you really asking? I've shared with you over the past few years how my spirituality and understanding of God is changing. My faith is stronger than it ever has been, and my relationship to the Divine is the most fun I have experienced. I'm not rejecting as much as I'm understanding and accepting even more."

"But saying 'the Divine' sounds like you're rejecting God and all of the ways God has been with us and guided us and how we've felt loved." All of a sudden, I was crying.

Softly, he explained, "The word 'God' also carries hurtful associations for me, from the times people have used God as a means to control and further their own agenda. We've both experienced that."

"Yes, but for me that was *people* who were harmful, not God."

"I agree, but the word 'God' is limiting to my awareness of things spiritual. I can't quite shake the connection to those 'God-in-a-box' Christians who want their worlds and God neat and tidy and require answers to all their questions. I understand that desire and need, but I have come to appreciate the mystery."

"And you have to do that with 'the Divine'?" My question came out more sarcastic than I expected.

He smiled in acknowledgment of my attitude. "For me, 'The Divine' encompasses the expansiveness of Spirit in a way that 'God' does not. 'God' is limiting to me, but 'the Divine' feels unrestrained. I feel more in sync with that term." He searched my eyes. "What's really going on for you?"

"It feels like you're rejecting a big part of our lives, and you've been changing so much—most of it good—and maybe I'm a little afraid you will reject *me* in all these changes."

He stepped over a pile of dark clothes and enfolded me in his arms. "I love you. You are a big part of the reason I've grown and am enjoying life now more than ever. I don't want to be without you."

I relaxed in his hug. "I don't want to give up 'God.'"

"You don't have to. I'm doing this for my benefit."

"Okay." I should have quit right there. "But do you know how arrogant and pretentious you sound?"

He let go of me, swept the laundry basket into his arms, and turned to leave. "Then you will have to decide if that's who I really am."

The ball of responsibility bounced right back into my court. My heart rate quickened. *Whoosh!* How could I go from feeling so close one moment to feeling alone with my own rude self for company? Why did I wreck such an intimate moment with a snarky comment?

It wouldn't be my last invitation to check that out.

4
Anxiety

"My best friends are people who share their anxious moments and worst fears as generously as they share their talents and competence. It's the open sharing by both parties that, for me, keeps the relationship balanced and intimate."
—Harriet Lerner

Early September

We now have three chemotherapy treatments behind us, and we're beginning to fall into a routine. Either Marci or I drop Reuel at the clinic where he goes to the chemo room and gets prepped for the eight-hour IV drip of toxins into his bloodstream. Today, Reuel tells me later, his good friend Harry brought lunch to him, and they shared a gourmet sandwich while they caught up with each other. The chemo doesn't create side effects for a day or two, so his appetite was good. Harry shared about the ongoing dynamics of the small business he runs, got Reuel's input about how to strategize the employee conflicts, and Reuel got Harry's input about the latest economic picture. Harry only planned to stay for an hour, but before they knew it, the IV bags had emptied, and four hours had passed.

After I pick up Reuel and he tells me about the visit with Harry, we have a soft, easily digestible meal together; tonight's menu is chicken soup. Then we strategize for the next week, since he may not feel like having another conversation for the next few days. The following morning, Reuel looks a queasy yellowish-green, which lasts for three days before he begins to feel better. This is common; he sometimes is nauseated, but mostly he gets weak and lethargic. The next week he returns to work, and by the third week you'd never know he has cancer. By the fourth week, we start the routine all over again.

Just before the fourth chemotherapy treatment, Reuel is scheduled for an MRI to see what effect the "friendly toxins" are having on the tumors, so I stay with him to get the results. Reuel jokes with the staff and asks Jim, the nurse, how he's been doing, then we wait in the room where we first got the news of his lymphoma diagnosis. I compare this visit to that experience. It's not as tense, but I have to focus on taking steady breaths. Reuel is humming, something he's always done no matter where he is, sometimes to my chagrin.

"Remember the neighbor in D.C. who cut my hair?" I ask him.

"Yeah?" His eyebrows knit together.

"Remember one of the first times she cut your hair? She heard you humming and thought you were coming on to her. She didn't know what to do—this new neighbor, and you were the young minister from the church next door. She asked, 'Are you serenading me?' You weren't even aware you were humming!" We smile at the memory.

Suddenly, after all these years, I realize that Reuel's humming helps calm his nervousness. I'm dumbstruck that I only just now recognize it. Then we hear the rustle outside the door that signals the doctor is about to enter. We take each other's hands.

The oncologist greets us with the usual chit-chat, and I want nothing to do with it. Just give us the results. Finally, he opens the chart.

"The results of your MRI are very encouraging. The chemotherapy treatment has shrunk many of the tumors on the spine, and it looks like one has disappeared completely." He looks up from the chart and smiles at us.

The held breath audibly whooshes out of our chests. My eyes close. I keep repeating the words in my head. Shrunk. Disappeared. *Then I look at Reuel. His eyes are damp, like mine, and we wish the doctor wasn't here.* Oh, who cares! *We hug, kiss, high five. We are euphoric.*

The oncologist is now our best friend. He had been right: Reuel does have a good chance at beating this! The chemo nurse comes to get Reuel situated, we hug once more, and I go to my office to update our Listserv of friends with the latest news. How fun it will be to write this update. Only five more chemotherapy treatments to go, and today we've gone from anxiety to elation. Maybe we can start planning a celebratory cruise.

....

 Inside Look: Marriage & Family Therapy Course Classroom, St. Paul, Mid-Career

"All right, class. I got feedback from several of you last week that you have many more questions about anxiety. Specifically, you want to know how it impacts the marriage, and even yourself, when you're counseling a couple. I might even wonder if you're a little 'anxious' about it. (Gotcha!) I can understand your confusion, because anxiety is a complex thing. Think of all the ways it shows itself: pre-game jitters, mouth-drying terror, a momentary flash, or a constant state of dread. What I've learned, both personally and professionally, is that anxiety drives more of our actions than we realize. Let me give you an example.

"Back when we were first married, my husband was totally scatterbrained. I would come home to find the loaf of bread in the laundry room, the checkbook in the refrigerator, and the quart of milk on the window-sill. At first it tickled me, and because it didn't happen all the time, I wasn't too worried he had dementia. After a while, though, when he lost countless pairs of shoes because he left them on the roof of the car as we drove off on weekend trips, or locked himself out of the house or car—one time with the car running—his lack of focus got really irritating, not to mention expensive. What we didn't realize until decades later is that his lack of focus was a symptom of PTSD. That anxiety from past trauma, when triggered, led to his loss of focus. I was the opposite. If my anxiety was triggered, I got quiet and went into hyper-observer mode, or else I would check out of the situation by daydreaming.

"Now, we didn't realize at the time that we were anxious. There were no panic attacks, no swooning, no facial tics, no throwing up. The reason we were clueless about it was that it felt 'normal.' We grow up absorbing whatever levels of anxiety are around us, as well as how others cope with it. The absentmindedness and daydreaming may be relatively harmless, but let's think about all the other responses to anxiety that can become problems. I'll make a list on the board . . ."

On the chalkboard, I write as they call out: hurt-ful remarks, avoiding going home, focusing only on the children or the pets, picking fights, withdrawing, physical aggression, and internal shame attacks.

"And here, class, is the most important point: all those examples of anxiety will end up in the therapy room with you and the couple. Your job is to notice it, manage your own reactions to it, and not let the anxiety seize control of the therapy! Once you help couples understand the sources of their anxiety, they become more aware and then have choices, versus reactions. Any questions?"

<hr />

Whenever we accept an invitation to intimacy, we deal with anxiety. The invitation to be vulnerable, whether we're on the extending or receiving end of the invitation, automatically raises anxiety. That's not "wrong;" it's just the nature of intimacy. However, if we don't recognize our anxiety, and don't understand its source, then we may misinterpret what to do with what we're feeling. And that, in turn, could keep us stuck in the shallow end of the intimacy pool or prevent us from jumping into the pool altogether.

Our brains are hardwired to react to anxiety by avoiding it. That works well for known dangers, like entering dark alleys or making a presentation to your boss when you're woefully unprepared. It doesn't work so well for creating or deepening intimacy, and it has taken me years to understand that what we avoid only grows stronger. Not only that, but whatever it is we repeatedly avoid then goes underground, out of our awareness, where it gains strength. Before we know it, we are inadvertently controlled by our anxiety, often without realizing it may be behind the wheel, driving us in ways we're not aware of or don't understand.

One of the first times I waded deeper into the intimacy pool occurred early in our marriage when Reuel was in seminary, and I worked the lunch and dinner shifts at the local country club. He innocently asked me to make his lunches to take to school. Internally, I bristled. *He has more time at home than I do. Why should I make his lunch? Because I'm the woman? Humph.* The honest response would have been to share my reactions, but I thought that to be likeable, I couldn't say no. Saying "No" in my family was not, shall we say, met with approval and usually triggered parental anger. I avoided "No" because it was coated with anxiety, and so I said, "Yes." Sometimes I made his lunch, but sometimes I just never quite got around to it. This went on for several weeks. Reuel never knew if I would actually make his lunch after I said I would. He finally confronted me.

"If you don't want to make my lunch, why don't you just say so?"

It was a good and awful question that required me to feel my anxiety in order to figure out the answer. I took a deep breath when I landed on the answer. "Because you might be mad at me!"

"Well, what about when you say you'll make it and you don't? Don't I have feelings then?"

"Yeah, but I'd be at work when you found out, so I wouldn't have to see your reaction," I admitted.

"It's okay to say no to me," he explained simply.

What relief filled me! I had tolerated the anxiety of looking within, and Reuel gave me permission to be honest with

31

him, which evidently I needed to hear. I had avoided saying no, but hadn't realized my anxiety about an anger outbreak was really controlling how I interacted with Reuel. Knowing myself, then allowing Reuel to know me, and later hearing his gentle response, created a closeness I would never have anticipated (or maybe I would have done it earlier).

We got hooked on the closeness. We wanted more, or at least to have it as a main ingredient in our marriage. As time went by, we made gradual discoveries about what got in the way of closeness. In the beginning we didn't have words to label it "anxiety," but we realized that if we were afraid to share something with the other, it would eventually drive us apart, not together. And because the closeness was so compelling to us, we kept wading deeper into the intimacy pool. However, this was not a smooth, synchronized swimming kind of process. We moved forward in fits and false starts, often treading water until we broke through some invisible barrier so that we could feel close again.

We bumped into lots of those invisible barriers, and some bruised us more than others. Eventually, we caught on that the barriers were related to something which had gone underground, out of our awareness. If we approached the barrier, we got anxious, just like my avoidance of saying "No" was connected to an underground fear of someone being mad at me.

It gradually dawned on us that we could continue bumping into those barriers, nursing our bruises, or we could figure out where the barriers were. And that meant we would need to dive into our childhoods to see what it was that created such stress in the first place.

Reuel's humming and my daydreaming, as I told my class, were relatively harmless ways to deal with stress. The problem was that some of our ways to deal with anxiety—needed and developed as children—turned out to be not only unnecessary but in fact problematic in our marriage. For example, it was important for me as a child to learn how to please a rageful parent, but by the time I entered adulthood, the need to please was driving me. Reuel, on the other hand, learned early in life to criticize himself before his parents could criticize and punish him. But what once protected him took on a life of its own in adulthood and nearly did him in. What were once childhood survival skills, as I often tell my clients, morph into adult intimacy blockers.

Reuel's childhood, growing up on the island of Barbados as the youngest child of missionary parents, was characterized by loss. When he was four years old, his family had just completed a year-long furlough in the United States and boarded a plane to return to their Caribbean island home. His fourteen-year-old sister, to whom Reuel was most attached, remained in the States to live with another family during high school. No one thought to prepare this four-year-old for such a stark separation until the plane began to taxi down the runway.

"Where's Sissy?" he cried. "Where is she? Where's my sissy?"

As the plane gained speed, so did the volume and intensity of his cries. He knew something was desperately wrong. Sissy wasn't there, his parents weren't going to make it better, and his most solid attachment figure was being ripped from him.

The losses mounted as he left his friends every four years to spend a year in the States, then had to leave these new friends to return to Barbados. When Reuel was nine, he lost his fourteen-year-old brother to live with another family in the States. It also didn't help that his parents thought the best way to discipline was to take away his favorite toys, which might have brought him comfort.

When Reuel reached that pivotal age of fourteen, his parents informed him they were returning to the States for good. They didn't want to leave him behind (like they had his siblings) for his high school experience, so they would move back to the U.S., and his dad would find an American church to pastor. To Reuel's adolescent mind, they were ripping him away from his Barbados family, the ones who hugged him, played with him, nannied him, taught him to pick limes and herbs for the flying fish, showed him how to bellyboard, and loved him in generous and unconditional ways.

I was aghast when Reuel first told me this—not only at the content, but at what happened to his body when he told me: shoulders back, stiff arms, stoic face, and unemotional tone for what I found to be a very disturbing story. But he wasn't finished.

"When I realized I was never returning to Barbados, I just decided I would only think about what was ahead. This part of my life was over. I told myself to move on. I would no longer be friends with these people because I couldn't see them anymore."

"You never talked to them again? Never wrote?"

"No. It was like a switch was flipped. I learned that everything is disposable. Nothing is permanent—not where you live, the house, the country you live in, not who your friends are, where you go to school, not even your family. Family can be left anywhere, anytime, for any reason deemed acceptable by parents. Children have no say in the matter; they must obey or be punished."

Reuel's survival skill was clear-cut. To avoid feeling the pain of all those losses, he had to shut down internally. That was a successful strategy in the short term, because it helped him survive in a rigid family system. However, in the long term, because the experiences of losing what he most cherished so branded his heart, he developed a sense of impending doom that hung over him. It wasn't visible to others, and most people would have been surprised at the dark cloud he carried. Even I wasn't privy to all the occasions he weathered the foreboding internal storms, but eventually, the building pressure had to break. He cherished me, but the lesson he absorbed in childhood was that the things he most loved, he lost. That's what was behind his intense reaction to the late return from my day with Janet when he was ready to call the State Patrol. His anxiety about losing me had begun to to drive him and infiltrate our marriage. His anxiety was blocking our intimacy.

My childhood, growing up in the Pacific Northwest, looked very different from Reuel's. Probably, my hard-wiring was loaded from the outset to be compliant and easygoing, the kind of kid who got invited to lots of birthday parties. Friends of my parents who were single or childless asked to take me to the Rose Festival Parade or to see the Christmas windows at Meier & Frank department store. I was a good sample child for parenting, so they checked me out like a library book and returned me to my parents afterwards. If the friends thought I was likeable, then my parents wouldn't get mad at me. Their anger was to be avoided at all costs. If my parents were mad, then my body flooded with anxiety because, like too many children, I unknowingly believed that my survival depended on my parents liking me, on their not getting angry.

Around second grade, though, I found a new thing to be worried about. What I saw in my parents didn't ring true to what they said aloud. I saw Daddy at church with Brother Brown, laughing and acting like the best of friends, but when he got in the car to drive home, he was full of bad words about Bro. Brown. When Sister Steele called with a prayer request, Mommy acted very concerned in her soft, caring voice, but after she hung up, she called Sis. Steele a "gossip" in her hard, tired voice. When I was ten years old, Daddy told me he got a surprise speedboat for Mommy, whom we all knew hated the water. We would keep it a secret, he said. I was thrilled that we now had a boat, but also alarmed. I knew, even at that young age, that the boat was really for Daddy, not Mommy. And I also knew that mommy would act happy because that's what daddy wanted. They weren't honest. I was deeply hurt and confused.

Such pain, and such a dilemma! I had to both avoid the hurt of parental dishonesty and find a way to know what was true or real. So in order to survive, I became a second-grade skeptic. I no longer automatically accepted what they said as truth. I searched for alternate explanations and watched for inconsistencies in their stories or behavior. I didn't dare question my parents about the inconsistencies—that would surely have resulted in their anger. I avoided their anger but also avoided airing my truth. Instead, I relied on my skepticism or early critical-thinking skills to determine what was real and avoided the terror of trusting someone who would let me down by not being honest.

Those were effective survival skills in the short term. Over time, however, the chronic avoidance of sharing my truth and an automatic skepticism began to create problems in our marriage. First, the longer my truth was buried, the more it became a stranger to me. If I didn't know myself, how could Reuel fully know me? Wham! Intimacy blocked. Second, my long-held skepticism had warped into a lack of trust in Reuel.

It was a fairly minor thing that brought this "un-trust issue" to a head. We were getting ready to go to a funeral, and I was putting the finishing touches on my hair. I picked up the hair spray to cement it in place when Reuel saw a piece out of place. He started to smooth it down when I jerked away from his hand. He, in turn, drew back and stared at me.

"That's it! I'm done. You refuse to accept my help or to believe that I see something you don't." He turned his back to walk away, then stopped. "I'm tired of my opinion not being as valid as everyone else's. You are more willing to believe someone at work, or even a stranger at the grocery store, than you are me. You don't trust me, and I'm not ignoring it any longer or pretending it doesn't hurt." Then he walked away. Of course, the first thing I did was check my hair. He was right! It did need smoothing.

He was also right that my early survival skills were creating blocks to our intimacy. As were his. It's probably just as well we didn't know all the blocks that were ahead. And we were fortunate that intimacy so captivated and motivated us. Not only would we need to withstand the anxiety of avoidance in the coming years, but we would need to withstand the anxiety of facing anxiety.

5
Truths

"'You are not who I thought you were' is one of the most painful realizations that lovers come to, and this is inevitable in any relationship, because no one is ever who we think they are."
— Chelsea Wakefield

Third Week of November
It's the week before Thanksgiving, almost time for the seventh chemo treatment. Reuel is feeling better than he has in months, even better than before the diagnosis. He just completed another MRI, and this time we can't wait to hear how positive the results are. We're counting down the weeks until treatment ends, and he's recovered enough to take a celebration cruise.

We are enjoying a rare evening at home together, Reuel watching the History Channel and I modifying our holiday menu because Reuel will have just had chemo the Monday before. The phone rings. Reuel answers, signals to me it's the oncologist, and clicks on the speaker. My heart rate increases. This is never a good sign.

"I have the results of the MRI, and I was taken completely by surprise," he begins. Another surprised doctor is a bad sign. "This MRI looks nothing like the first one. Some of the tumors that

had shrunk have grown back, and now there are also some new ones growing at an alarming rate."

We are stunned into silence. Finally Reuel asks, "What does this mean?"

"Sometimes," the doctor says, "the chemotherapy quits working. We don't know why that happens, but it sometimes does. It's like the body builds a resistance to it."

"But I feel so good," Reuel says.

"You have gotten some immediate relief from the initial benefits of the chemotherapy, but other tumors are growing."

"What do we do? Do I try a different chemo on Monday?"

"No, no more outpatient chemotherapy. We must be very aggressive with our treatment. You will now need to be hospitalized, because the chemicals will be harsher in order to try to arrest the growth of the bone metastases."

I want to ask a question, but I don't know which. "Hope?" is all that comes out of my mouth.

"Yes, there's always hope, but we must act aggressively. We don't know why the chemo quit working. It sometimes just happens," he repeats.

So this is what that term "sucker punched" means. Truth hurts. We look at each other with mouths open and heads shaking. I feel like I might throw up. Questions flash through my mind, and I'm sure Reuel's mind, so fast we don't even have time to ask them.

We alternate bursts of short questions for the doctor, each beginning with "But—" They spring from a sense of betrayal, injustice, unreality. Finally, the call ends.

We have done everything right. Reuel is a good patient. We are a good and supportive family team. We have incredible support from our community of friends. Reuel's attitude is positive and so are

the attitudes of those around him. That's all we ever allow. We have
all drawn closer together and deeper in our spiritual relationship.
This is entirely unjust, and please, no one dare to tell me that life is
unfair. We're in a whole different category here.

....

Inside Look: My Counseling Office, Minneapolis, Mid-Career

"It must have been devastating for you, Sam, to learn about John's secret gambling life in the casinos. And John, it must have been equally upsetting for you to learn about Sam's secret shopping habits."

"How could he do this to me, to our kids? He's gambled away their college funds!" Sam looks toward where John is crumpled on one end of the couch with the Kleenex box.

"Well, what about you? You could start your own shopping network with what's in our basement!" John is now so agitated he looks like he could spring out the door.

"Okay," I interrupt, "let's take a breath here. You have every right to the feelings you have, but now that the truth is out on the table, we're going to have to figure out how to move forward in constructive ways. You can keep beating each other up with your words if you want, but it will distract you from the core issue: dealing with the truth."

"What do you mean?" Sam asks, and I'm not sure which of them looks most skeptical.

"Like every couple, the two of you have to reconcile your differences in dealing with truth. Somehow you told yourselves that it was okay to keep secret these major things you were doing. Maybe it started small and snuck up on you, like many addictions do. But somewhere along the way, you quit saying what was true and started to hide things. And my guess is that there's a lot more than gambling or shopping addictions that you're hiding. If your relationship is to survive, as you say you want, then you'll need to decide if you're ready for truth—from yourselves and from each other."

One of the hardest times to be a marriage therapist is sitting with a couple when one spouse reveals some horrifying truth to the other. Sometimes we as therapists know or have a gut feeling that a secret is about to be exposed, but other times we're as surprised as the unknowing partner. The shock grenade explodes the secret affair, the covert drinking, or coming out as queer, and all of us in the room reel from the concussion of new or open information. Sometimes it feels like the oxygen has been sucked from the room, and we're all flapping about like fish on a hot dock. Other times it feels like a wave of relief has washed over the couple to finally have the secret out and on the table where it can be dealt with. Whether the truth is sudden or has been slowly building, it creates a new reality which requires a reworking of the couple's relationship.

When one partner is deciding whether to reveal their secret, they often ask me whether I think their marriage could "handle the truth." That is always a tough call, because so much of the answer depends on how well a partner can deal with the pain of the truth. Will they be overwhelmed to the point of permanent collapse? Or get stuck in the blame game and never move on? Or is there enough of a strong, core self within each that allows them to recover from hearing the truth and create a better marriage? Sometimes the grenade of truth explodes the relationship into pieces that can't be put back together. What does seem certain is that any long-term marriage or partnership doesn't escape the consequences of hiding the truth. Even when the spouses have colluded in some way—usually nonverbally and nonconsciously—to not tell or not hear the truth, there are consequences. Then a new truth emerges (to keep the secret), and the relationship organizes around the new truth.

In our own marriage, we had to deal with both sudden—like a cancer diagnosis—and slow-forming truth grenades. I learned first-hand that the slow-forming grenades can still jerk you into a new reality. And often, embedded in those grenades (or maybe in the shrapnel?), is the invitation to a deeper intimacy.

From everything I experienced, our marriage was thriving. Reuel experienced a level of safety with me that he had never felt before, and he began to let his guard down and enjoy life more. I learned to let Reuel see my hurts, because I trusted him, and I flourished under his attention. My confidence grew, and my self-esteem increased. The more we knew each other—body, mind, and spirit—the more grounded we felt in our marriage.

The problem, I learned years later, was that he often put his own needs and hurts aside while he tended to my pain. To my chagrin, I was not as generous to Reuel.

How is it that the behaviors we despise in a parent—like my dad's self-centeredness—are the very ones that lie hiding in our subterranean levels? The more giving Reuel was, the more I took. He believed it was his job to make me happy, and who was I to argue? I was the one who decided where we went to eat on our Friday night dates, how we spent the weekend, which couples we socialized with. I kept pushing the limits of Reuel's giving until I read his displeasure, usually in a nonverbal clue of anger, impatience, or withdrawal. Then I would ask about *his* preferences, what *he* wanted for the weekend, made sure *his* sexual needs were met. I would have been dumbfounded had anyone suggested I was behaving like my father (or my mother). After all, Reuel and I were always kind in our interactions. We were neither aggressive nor demanding, but for a long time the smelly truth was that I disproportionately received from Reuel. He was caretaking my feelings just the way I had my father's. It was only when the scale tipped toward displeasing him that I would return to my mother's role of caretaking his feelings. Between us there was nothing blatant, nothing hostile, just a rhythm that seemed part of our marital dance, and we prided ourselves on being much better dancers than the couples around us.

We continued in this seemingly benign marital rhythm through the stages of raising our children in what I thought, and Reuel often declared, was a good marriage. But years later, after our kids were gone and Reuel was in therapy, he realized just how much he had not been saying his own truth. This from a man who, I was convinced, always spoke his truth. A slow-forming truth grenade was about to explode.

He explained it this way: "I didn't have the courage to tell you what I really wanted, or how much I wanted it, or when I thought things only went your way. What I was used to from childhood was getting yelled at, blamed, or being left."

"Did you think that's what I would do, too?"

He shook his head yes, with pain in his eyes but also kindness. "I'm not sure I had the courage to see for myself what I was doing. That wasn't fair to you, and it wasn't fair to me."

I was floored. Mostly. I think some part of me knew this and kept it tucked away out of awareness. Here was this man, a truth-teller unlike anyone I had known, and he hadn't been telling me the truth? My mind flashed to various clients whose relationships didn't survive an explosion of reality.

Could I possibly tolerate all this truth?

The grenade had detonated, but for some reason I was not paralyzed by shame at Reuel's revelation. I could accept truth. Perhaps I knew by then that honesty in our relationship, no matter how painful, always had a healing and liberating purpose. I knew he wasn't intentionally inflicting pain. He wanted something more for both of us, and he realized he had to be more honest with himself and me.

His truth didn't come gushing, but seeped out, like a slow drip. It was nerve-wracking. My gut twisted with dread during this period whenever Reuel said he wanted to talk or I opened an unexpected email from him. Would this be the time he was too worn out to keep working on the marriage? Would he decide it's too hard to make important changes and call it quits? Or an even more startling thought, would *I* decide to quit? Would he tell me there were yet more truth grenades to detonate? I was happy in our marriage, but I wondered if I'd been living with an imposter, someone who hadn't been honest. That possibility ripped through me. *Maybe*, I thought, *it would be easier to quit.*

No! That can't be the solution for us! I wasn't willing to surrender what I knew deep in my heart was a profoundly life-giving intimacy we each had experienced. Reuel may not have been fully transparent with me through the years, but I knew we had something of substance. There had to be a way to move through this pain and confusion to a better place. I chose to take another look inside to see what was on my side of the fence. And that is when my own truth began to seep into my awareness, a torturous trickle of conceding to the ways I was like my father. After one particularly painful recognition about how withholding and ungenerous I had been, I wondered if Reuel would think I was worth the effort and energy to work through these issues. I was terrified to ask him, but more terrified not to ask.

"I feel so bad for those times I have shut you out. I, I don't even know how you could love me," I sobbed.

He was quiet for an agonizingly long time. Finally, he said, "Yes, I do love you, and yes, this is also very painful for me. I didn't know it would require so much strength to tell you my truth and for us to deal with it."

I felt enormous relief that he still loved me, but he wasn't finished.

"I have to work hard to stay in the present, because if I look to the past to predict the future, then I get afraid nothing will change, that it is hopeless for us to have a different marriage."

I wanted to offer hope. "But isn't what we're doing right now a change, with you telling me your truth, and me hearing it and feeling your pain? Isn't that something different than what we've done before?"

"Maybe. There's a part of me that wants to punish you for all the times I've felt alone." He spoke rapidly then, brow furrowed. "You may want to be closer to me now, but what about all those previous times?"

"But how was I supposed to know about those times when you never told me?" I felt desperate.

"I know that, but I'm angry. I wanted you to know why I hurt. You were supposed to protect me from hurt, not cause it."

"What? Protect you—?"

"I know, I know. You are not my mother."

Whew. Thank God he knows that.

He paused, seemingly to collect his thoughts. "I know this anger comes from a time before we were even together. It's because I was so hurt back then. But later, at times when I felt hurt by you, I got angry and wanted to make you a target."

"Okay…" I wasn't sure what to say to that. We were quiet for several moments, looking more at the floor than anywhere else. Then Reuel put his hand on my leg, and I looked at him.

"I still believe in us. I still believe more in the strength that moves us to healthy places than in the anger and hopelessness that can blow us apart. It's a strange time in our lives, but I believe we are both doing our best to stand beside each other."

"I believe we are, also. And"—I took a big breath—"I

think we need to keep asking for what we need."

He nodded. "And," he paused to look deep into my eyes, "I do love you."

If intimacy is indeed to know and be known, then Reuel's truth grenade thrust us to a new level of knowledge about each other and ourselves, an invitation that felt more like a concussion than a warm hug. Just how many levels of intimacy would we need to descend before we could get back to the blissful highs?

6
Trust

"Building trust in a relationship requires taking risks together that show us our partner isn't the same as the people from our past who hurt us. Most importantly, trust requires taking risks together that help us grow into better partners for each other."
—Esther Perel and Mary Alice Miller

Fourth Week of November

It's Tuesday morning about a week after the doctor's phone call. I don't have a client until noon, although I had planned to go to the office early to get caught up on paperwork. Reuel has time off work because we thought he would be in the throes of chemo right now. When I look at him leaning against the kitchen island, face drawn and hand tight around his coffee cup, I change my mind about the office.

"How are you doing?" I ask.

"Ooooh, not so good," he replies, his eyes tearing.

"Are you in pain?"

"No. Well, not physically." A long pause while he looks into his coffee. He finally looks up. "I'm really scared."

I set down my mug and go to him, wrapping my arms around his waist, snugging my head against his chest. I love the way our bodies mesh when we hug, the way his tall frame surrounds me, his chin fitting on the top of my head. Suddenly I'm scared too. What if I don't have this body to hug anymore? I squeeze him more fiercely. Our usual way of blocking out the fear by focusing on the healing is not working this morning. After a while, I break the silence.

"Do you want to go into the Flow?"

Flow is the term Reuel applied to describe his experience of not just prayer, but of a dialogue and mutual interaction with the Divine. He learned that during these times of intense prayer, he was in such an altered state that he didn't always remember everything that transpired, so he would ask me to transcribe his interactive prayer onto paper. I document both Reuel's prayers and what he hears back from the Divine. We used to question whether Reuel was making it up. We resolved the question many months ago when we realized that the truth of those times in the Flow stands on its own, no matter the source.

"Yes. No. I need to. I want to, but I'm scared to even go into the Flow." His voice was small.

I've never heard him say he's afraid to go into the Flow. I make my mind up. "All the more reason for us to do it," I say, pushing him up the stairs ahead of me. I sound more confident than I feel.

Up in our bedroom, we take our corners on the king-sized bed, Reuel propped by a back rest at the foot of the bed, I mirroring his position at the headboard. We've done this enough that I keep a tablet in my nightstand, which I retrieve along with a pen. I find myself in awe, slightly terrified at this surreal experience every time I witness Reuel being in the Flow while I record the words that come out of his mouth. I wait on Reuel, who finally closes his eyes and opens his prayer by acknowledging how afraid he is.

He is quiet. I am quiet. The house and the neighborhood are quiet. And then he begins an anguished dialogue, my pen flying across the page to keep up.

". . . I thought I knew the truth, but the direction things are going doesn't seem consistent with truth. I'm doubting truth because of the initial message that I had cancer, but I'll survive. Was that me or the Divine?. . . So the attacks on my spirit have been trying to confuse me about what truth is. The truth is that I was never told it was a clean, simple process from Point A to Point B.

"I've always been afraid of dying because of other people's mistakes. The truth is I almost did die. My life was threatened by the neglect and mistakes of people. I don't want to have to die again because of others' mistakes.

"The message is coming at a time I feel the weakest. It's more difficult to let in. As if the Divine wants to carry me . . . part of me is afraid of being carried. I want to be. But I want to be carried further in this life, not out of this life. Not yet."

My hand struggles to keep up. Reuel's eyes are shut tight, his face tilted as if he's straining to hear.

Reuel says, "The response back to me is:

'Just. Accept.'

"Accept what?" Reuel pauses, processing.

"'Accept being carried.'

"I have to let go and accept the Divine carrying me. The Divine wishes it.

'That requires trust.'

"How much trust do I have to give in this life?

'Just enough. Enough is the trust you're given. You trust Judy enough. Then you can trust me enough.'

"Yes.

'The lack of guarantee is an obstacle for you.'

"Yes." *Reuel nods.*

> "'Guarantees and trust are not the same. Trust is stronger than guarantees. For human nature, it is counterintuitive. You didn't trust you could do this—go into the Flow—but this is what you were given. Trust is stronger than anything.'

"But isn't it weak?" *Reuel's forehead crinkles.*

> "'Humans weaken trust by doubt, by wanting guarantees. But trust is stronger. Do you trust you will live?'

"I've lost trust in recent days.

> 'I know. And it's okay.'

Through tears, Reuel continues, "To hear those words from you—it's amazing. So calm, so opposite of what evil tells me. There's no retribution, no payback, no death sentence. I dearly and desperately want to trust because I want to live. One of your early followers said, 'Lord I believe; help my unbelief.' It would seem dishonest to say anything other than 'I trust and have moments of distrust.'"

There is a long silence. "The best part of me is when I trust. The best part of Judy and me is when we're trusting. But I don't trust perfectly. . . . Help me trust more purely and perfectly.

> 'I will.'

"That seems like all for now.

> 'It is. For now. But come back again.'"

We come back into the room. I mention to Reuel that this has got to be the opposite experience from formal, ritualized prayers in organized religious services. He nods in agreement.

"Do you see why I'm careful who I tell about these times? How do you describe this without sounding arrogant or psychotic?"

"Yeah," *I smile.* "These times are like divine intimacies. It's the ultimate communion."

Inside Look:
Minneapolis Counseling Office, Mid-Career

"I can't believe you think I don't trust her! I know Susan has never cheated on me!"

"And I know Ron has never had an affair! I think you're wrong about us not trusting each other, and that makes me wonder how much you can really help us."

Whoo-boy. I should be used to the strong reactions couples have whenever I challenge them that they may not be trusting each other. I take another stab at it.

"It's good you have so much confidence in each other's faithfulness. That's a strength! But trust involves so much more than sexual fidelity. Trust has to do with the ways you believe your spouse and allow him or her to influence you."

I wait to see if they are with me. They both maintain eye contact, so I continue. "Trust may be giving each other the benefit of the doubt or assuming the best from the other. It's pretty much the opposite of contempt, and I already told you how Gottman found contempt to be the 'battery acid' of relationships." Susan and Ron nod their heads.

"Destroying trust through cheating or having an affair is devastating, but that's not the only way a betrayal of trust shows up."

"I need an example." Ron rarely asks for more in our sessions.

"Well," I scramble for specifics . . . "Lies, secrets, making things look different than they are, and sharing with others beyond what your spouse feels comfortable with." I see them taking that in but realize I need to get even more specific to their own marriage. I need to call them out on problems they mentioned last session. "Sometimes we undermine trust by withdrawing approval, demanding perfection, or by refusing to give the benefit of doubt."

They look stung. Their glances at each other suggest they also recognize they have been the sting-ers as well as the sting-ees. That is progress, but I wonder if they will continue to let the recognition sink in.

For far too long, I didn't understand how I violated trust in my own marriage without ever having an affair. Reuel told me the same was true for him.

....

I'm pretty good at paying attention. Maybe we all are pretty good at it, but what we each attend to can be quite different. My brother-in-law, for example, was excellent at paying attention to where the largemouth bass were lurking in the local rivers and lakes. My cousin's boy could name every make, model, and year of each car we passed on the freeway. My daughter wouldn't have a clue about fishing holes or makes of cars, but she pays attention to photo opportunities and precise color saturation of the finished photo.

Reuel paid attention to those times when he knew that he knew something, to his intuition, and how to act on his knowledge. In our early marriage, he paid attention to his knowing that he wasn't ready to leave seminary after three years, so he stayed an extra year to get his degree in counseling. That decision eventually changed the course of his career. Later, he knew he needed healing for his emotional pain, so he sought help. As a result, he grew more relaxed within himself and was lots more fun to be around. He paid attention to his knowledge that he was anxious about money, that something was unbalanced there. Eventually, he realized his over-control of finances wasn't working. Much to my relief, he decided to let go of his worry about financial security and to trust that we could figure it out together. Thanks to his paying attention to his anxiety and letting it go, I also got to relax more, since his peace was as contagious as his anxiety had been.

Sometimes he would experience a knowing about a client situation. Once, we were at a friend's house making a Nigerian dinner together. Reuel was in the midst of learning to make fufu, when he looked up and declared he had had an insight about a client couple I was working with. He motioned me outside for a "consultation." My friend describes looking out the kitchen window at us, Reuel intensely sharing his understanding, punctuated with waving arms, me looking up at him, deeply listening. His insight was right on. It shifted my clinical progress with the couple in a positive direction.

His sense of knowing was not always welcomed or accepted by me, nor was it always accurate. More than once we came to an impasse of differing perspectives. One gridlock occurred over two friends of mine about whom Reuel had strong negative feelings. It wasn't just that he didn't like these friends—he actually had some enjoyable social times with them—but also he had a sense of knowing that each had an ulterior motive in the relationship. At first, he had a hard time describing it.

"I'm really concerned about you getting together with them. Something is off," he began.

"What do you mean?"

"I'm not really sure, but there's something different in how they relate to you. It's not a good feeling."

"I haven't picked up on any of that."

"Well, what is it you enjoy about them?"

"I really like our conversations, the intellectual stimu- lation and creativity, and each of them has a different way of looking at the world." I saw his face sag. "What's going on?"

"I think each of them is attracted to you, and I don't trust either of them."

I was thunderstruck. "Really?"

"Yes, and that you're so surprised concerns me," he said. "I think you're not in touch with yourself when it comes to sexual attraction."

"What?" I started a slow burn. "So is it them you don't trust, or is it me?"

He didn't answer. "Would you just consider my con- cerns?"

"It seems to me that I would know if there was some- thing to be concerned about," I fired back at him. Then I took aim: "Are you feeling threatened in some way?"

His jaw tightened, but I had more to say. "My friend- ship with Zach is deeper than with Wanda, but she and I have more in common educationally. So I enjoy meeting each of them for lunch now and then. You may not have friends like that, so you don't understand."

He chose his words carefully. "I just sense a predator vibe to each of them, in different ways, and I want you to know that."

"Okay." Irritated, I left the room. I grabbed the laundry basket and started to fold clothes as an outlet. *I've always been more social and had more friends than he has,* I thought, flicking the wrinkles out of a t-shirt. *Maybe he's socially underdeveloped and just doesn't get it. Maybe he's jealous. I get to pick my own friends. Where does he get off trying to control me?* I looked around. The laundry was folded faster than my anger could drain away.

We came back to discuss this topic again, after we had dealt with our own thoughts and feelings. I wondered how to respect my own thoughts and feelings about these friends and still respect Reuel's. In my mind, I argued a moral high ground about boundaries, individuation, and his need for further maturity. At least I thought I'd contained it to my thinking, but it spilled out one night in another discussion. This time Reuel took a more heated and intense position.

"How is it that *I'm* the villain? Is it because I'm naming things, or because I won't let it drop?"

"I never said you were a villain." I hoped I sounded reasonable and calm. "We just have different opinions."

"My sense about them—that something is not right—is as strong as ever. But as a result of these discussions, I have pulled back in a different way."

"What do you mean?" I was caught between anxiety and relief.

"I no longer trust your judgment as it relates to these two people. What I have seen is that you go through some kind of intellectual process to re-interpret, set aside, and then dismiss my concerns."

He interrupted me before I could begin. "Just wait. When you go through that process to dismiss my concerns, you turn me into the bad guy. That way if your point is proven, my concerns are dismissed, and you get to keep the relationships. My question is, why go to all that mental work just to maintain these relationships?"

"I don't see those relationships as the ones needing work," I retorted. "The hard part—the work—is between us!"

"Bingo! You talk about it being okay for you to see it one way and me another, and you call it differentiation. But I know now that regardless of your words, you believe that how I see it is simply wrong, and your view is accurate and right. That lets you dismiss my real concerns. If the situation were reversed—"

I cut him off. "Whenever you use that argument, alarm bells go off inside me. You sound so self-serving when you say that, like you're so righteous that you would *never* do that to me. What is it that I'm doing to you?"

"I'm deeply hurt, insulted, and I feel denigrated."

The steam went out of me, and I got still.

"Could you just imagine for a moment," he continued, "that you had strong concerns about one of my friends and what you would expect of me when you expressed them?"

I felt trapped. I cared that he felt hurt, but I didn't want to be controlled by him. After a pause, I decided to be honest. "I would expect you to listen to me, to respect my concerns, and to begin moving away from the friend."

"Then why is your opinion more valuable than mine?" he asked, not with a "gotcha" tone, but with pain. I had no good response. It hurt me that I had caused him so much hurt.

We sat in silence. It wasn't the first time I had thought about how hard this part of marriage is. The question I kept returning to was: How do I respect Reuel and respect myself when our perspectives are so far apart? Does one of us have to "not count" for the other to be valued? At different times I had tried to manage the tension by explaining to myself and him that we just had different opinions and might have to agree to disagree. And sometimes that was true. But other times, like this one, that rationalization ignored each of our hurting hearts. Can we just dismiss the other's hurts as a difference in perspective, the cost of doing business in marriage?

Right then, the cost of dismissing hurts was too high a price in our marriage. I didn't like how cold I had to feel in order to set aside his ache. I wasn't even clear whether this encounter was a struggle for power or for integrity. The more I thought through these values, the clearer I got. These friends that he was so opposed to were not my partners for life. They were not family. I had no expectations of moving into the future with them, nor did we have much history together. How would it feel for me to withdraw from these friendships? Uncomfortable, a little awkward, but it wouldn't leave a deep scar. My priority was this husband who had loved me through three kids, growing pains, and a Ph.D.

Reuel glanced up at me. His words came haltingly. "I'm asking you to accept and respect the very clear sense I have about these people that there is tremendous imbalance in their lives. That imbalance is impacting you and our relationship, maybe more than you're able to sense at this time."

He must have seen on my face that I wanted to hear him now, so he continued. "You know how rarely I have felt this way about anyone. It may not make sense to you, but my sense of them is clear. I'm asking you to move away from those relationships."

There it was, the flat-out request. What really was the ground I was supposed to be defending? That I had the right to choose my own friends? We both knew I did. That wasn't the issue. The issue here was how important Reuel was to me, how much I valued our relationship, how much I trusted him, and the damage that would be done if I didn't respect his request. I was committed to him, to our past, to our shared future. I was clear at last.

"You are more important to me than those relationships. I love you. If it is causing you and us that much pain, I will move away from them. You are the one I cherish."

He looked at me, tears spilling from his eyes, and held out his arms. I went to him in two steps. We wrapped our arms around each other and held on.

There were no guarantees Reuel could give me that his "knowing" was correct. I had to trust him. Actually, I had to trust our relationship, that he was not out to stifle or control me. Instead, he asked for me to know him, to recognize his understanding, and to be influenced by that. It turned out he was inviting me to a deeper intimacy.

7
Doubt

"That's a powerful thing, knowing you can reveal yourself to someone. It made me want to be a better person."
—Roxane Gay

Last Week of November
Reuel is getting ready for his first inpatient chemo treatment. He had to say goodbye to his team at work since he's going on short-term disability. They have a hard time with what this may mean, and some of them get tearful whenever he gives them an update.

He told the clients in his private practice that his treatment is taking a different course, and he's unsure if he'll be able to meet with them regularly. He transferred some of them to other therapists, and others were ready to take a break from therapy. Some of them asked to be on hold until he was feeling well enough to see them. He is energized by doing therapy, and I wonder about the cumulative effect on him of saying goodbye to clients.

There's no doubt now that our lives have plunged into the whirlpool of cancer. Our routines are changing, and we live with an unsettledness that affects each of us differently. Reuel tracks medication doses and timing instead of clients. I now make all the grocery runs and put gas in the cars. I've taken to holding my breath when I enter the house because I don't know if he will be incapacitated with pain or happily fixing dinner. Reuel, the self-diagnosed dyslexic who hates writing, tries journaling his experience but loses focus. Almost every drive home from the office now includes a stop at the pharmacy to pick up the latest pain or nausea relief or iron-boosting prescription.

Aaron and Cory are fairly removed from the action, one in Hawaii and the other in Manhattan, while Marci, who lives in an apartment near downtown Minneapolis, has unexpectedly become a stable and organizing force for us. She calls (without prompting!), talks to her dad about how he's doing, asks me if she can help with household chores, and surprises us with treats when she visits at the hospital. I am amazed to see this notorious procrastinator arrange her schedule around her work shifts to include hospital or home visits.

My client load remains at thirty-five sessions a week. I consider reducing my hours, but that seems more trouble than it's worth, especially if this next chemotherapy will halt the cancer. I realize that being present to each client means I don't have to think about lymphoma or its effects for a full fifty minutes. Between sessions, I ponder when to phone Reuel, since he might be sleeping, and heave a sigh with the effort of decision. As I lock the office for the night, I am torn between rushing home and dragging my feet with dread to see how Reuel is tolerating whatever is currently happening in his body.

As uncertain and scary as this whirlpool is, we still are confident Reuel will come through it okay. He just has to. His indomitable spirit will once again overcome, just as it has so many times previously. I don't doubt that. I must not doubt that.

Inside Look:
Minneapolis Counseling Office, Mid-Career

"Lucy, what happens when you doubt your husband?" I'm seeing Lucy individually this week after first meeting with her and her husband Terry for marital therapy. I'll see Terry by himself later in the week. Both have high-powered positions in their companies, and both say they want a better marriage, though they're not sure it's possible.

"I hate it!" cries this well-dressed corporate executive. "I get filled with uncertainty and it feels like I'm getting eaten alive by gnats. Why is doubting so difficult?"

"Probably because it forces us to hold two things that seem contradictory—belief and nonbelief. Mentally and emotionally, we have to make a place within us for the possibility of both yes and no, for being both certain and uncertain. We just don't like being in-between! I can understand why doubt is a risky thing in your job position when you need to be decisive, but what happens in your marriage when you doubt?"

"I pull back from Terry and go inside myself. I get very discouraged that things will never change. Sometimes I blame him and criticize everything he's doing. He can't do anything right when I'm doubting." She shakes her head.

"At those times, what exactly are you doubting?"

"Oh, good question . . . I've never asked myself that." She's silent for several moments. "I'm thinking about one of the times I doubted Terry, like when he made the decision to change jobs. If I'm really honest—and I've never thought about this before—it may be myself that I'm doubting, like whether I married the right man."

"And what's that like for you?"

"Terrible! I hate to think that. I don't like to be uncertain! I've advanced so far in my career because I've been decisive."

"Well, then, I may have bad news for you. Doubt is as much an ingredient of marriage as frustration or humor or figuring out who's going to do the dishes. It's what we do with our doubts that leads us into self-destruction or growth. When doubts are ignored or denied they don't disappear but instead grow underground, creating pressure as their shoots try to crack the surface of our consciousness. The pressure unbalances us."

"Yes! I feel totally unbalanced when I doubt Terry! I assume that pressure must mean something's wrong with our marriage." She leans forward, face tense. "What do we do?"

"Often what we do is try to rebalance by withdrawing or attacking. Or, we can acknowledge the doubts, take responsibility for them, and allow the doubts to lead us to new understanding."

....

Doubt can be a free-fall with no ripcord. Doubt can seep into our spirits and unbalance us until we wrap ourselves into cocoons of withdrawal or hurl prickly projectiles of defensiveness in an effort to find footing and safety. Doubt, at its extreme, can suck hope from the soul.

On the other hand, doubt can be valuable. How could a

jury ever find an accused innocent without reasonable doubt? How could science proceed without doubting a hypothesis? Could we arrive at any eventual truth without first having doubts?

This dialectic of doubt—having the potential for both value or destructiveness in its effect—feels awful. The internal teeter-tottering is uncomfortable. We have to hold, mentally and emotionally, that which seems contradictory: I believe, and I don't believe; I'm certain, and I'm not certain. We avoid making decisions when we are suspended between "yes" and "no."

Doubts, with all their potential for positive or negative effects, insert themselves into marriages, and then we are confronted with how to manage them. I thought I never doubted my decision to marry Reuel. Life with him was so immeasurably better than what I had experienced before that it never consciously occurred to me to doubt if he was "The One." Soon after we were married, however, I discovered that wasn't the case with our new friends Charles and Kari when Reuel recounted a conversation he'd had with Charles.

"Reuel," Charles asked one day when they were out together, "Kari says to me all the time that she wonders if she was supposed to marry me. Does Judy cry a lot?"

"Well, no. Not that I know, and our house is too small for me not to know."

"Kari cries herself to sleep more nights than not since we've been married. It tears me up inside. What have I done to make her so miserable? She told me 'That's just what wives do, once they get married, is cry themselves to sleep.' Is that what Judy does?"

Reuel and I were horrified that these friends were so miserable in their new marriage. They doubted each other, doubted themselves, doubted their own decision-making capacities. They were unable to tolerate the discomfort of doubts that probably began long before their wedding, and ultimately their marriage didn't survive.

I can trace some of my first doubts with Reuel. We had been dating steadily, not yet engaged, when we went to a costume party. He complimented me on my princess gown and told me I looked pretty, but his focus was more on the coed who converted her baby-doll nightgown to look like a roaring 20s flapper. Looking at the tall, leggy brunette, I doubted my own looks and ability to compete.

Years later, on a rare couple getaway before our tenth anniversary, we were relaxing at the beach when he saw me catch him as his eyes followed one of the shapely, exotic-eyed women out into the sea. We laughed, and he wanted me to be more open with him about the men I found attractive, because he believed that kind of mutual honesty helped "affair-proof" our marriage. I appreciated his authenticity—or told myself I did—but really, I didn't look anything like the women he was attracted to. I focused instead on valuing his honesty so I could downplay the doubts.

Reuel and I both tried to avoid our doubts for some time, frightened that they would be destructive to our marriage. Nowhere was this more clearly seen than in our sex life. For most couples, sex has a gravitational force that pulls all doubts and unresolved issues into its field. We were no different. Sex was a vehicle that drove us into new territory of confronting our doubts about ourselves and each other, and it eventually led us to some new truths. We were to travel much uncharted terrain in that vehicle before we were done.

I hated feeling doubt, but doubts in the sexual arena were the worst. Whenever Reuel's level of passion didn't match mine, he doubted first himself, then me. He shared his thought pattern with me: "Is something wrong with me? Is something wrong with Judy? Is she having an affair?"

I, on the other hand, doubted first Reuel, then myself. *Does he see everything as sexual? Does our wonderful day together become ruined for him if there's not sex? Maybe there is something wrong with me. I don't feel attractive, despite what Reuel tells me.*

We wrestled with some of these questions for years, not constantly, but often enough that we tried different ways to not feel the troubling doubts. They didn't work. Avoidance through withdrawing or blaming was our temporary fix. The resolution of doubts, we learned, took time and a willingness to meet the doubt head-on.

Somewhere between fifteen and twenty years of marriage, we had an encounter that started as a replay of our familiar, besieged sexual dance pattern but moved into new territory. We had returned from a full day of activities. I went upstairs to do my nightly rituals, then fell into bed and rolled away from Reuel. That was not what he had planned, and let me know it.

"Babe, what is going on?" Reuel implored. "Is it me? Am I oversexed or too passionate?"

"What do you mean? I'm just tired after our full day."

"We just spent a wonderful day together, and to me the perfect ending to this wonderful day is making love."

I was quiet and still. Then, somehow, I risked more honesty. "I just don't feel very attractive."

"What's going on for you? You have always been and still are the most attractive woman to me!"

"Well, when I see you looking at all these women who don't look like me, I tend to doubt my attractiveness. I feel like I just don't measure up!" My heart raced, surprised at the level of emotion I felt.

Reuel was surprised, also. "Uh, I thought we'd talked about this a long time ago. How long have you been feeling like this?"

"I don't know . . . a while. I've been wrestling with lots of doubts lately, maybe because of where I am in my Ph.D. program, so I've been trying to get to the bottom of all these doubts . . ."

Reuel burst into my explanation, voice raised. "Are you having an affair? Is that what the doubts are about and why you don't want to make love with me?" His face was drawn in pain.

"Me?" my voice caught. "Oh, no. No! That hasn't even occurred to me!" I waited, breath held, to make sure he believed me.

"Sorry." He reached for my hand. "I guess I am having my own doubts." We squeezed hands, and then I continued.

"In my head I know you appreciate me and find me attractive, but I think I started to doubt myself pretty early on in our relationship. I saw you look at other women when we were out. You never leered, and you didn't try to hide it from me, but I noticed your head turn. Whenever I asked about it, you honestly described what you found attractive."

"Okay . . ." Clearly, he didn't see the problem.

"It became a dilemma for me. I liked that you were being honest, even heard that honesty like that was good for a relationship. The problem was that the kind of women who turned your head looked nothing like me."

"But . . ."

"Just wait, I'm trying to get through this. And no, I didn't know I was going to talk about this tonight!" I took a deep breath. "Whenever I had uncertainties back then, I would talk my doubts down with positive messages about your honesty. But the doubts kept popping back up, even sometimes when you were appreciating me. On some level, I thought it was better to hide my inadequacies so I didn't have to feel such miserable self-doubt and shame." I folded my arms around me as some of the heat left my body. I felt Reuel's eyes on me and gradually looked at him.

"I'm so sorry you felt this way." His eyes began to water. Then I realized I needed to say more.

"Hang on. There's one other piece to this. I've only realized lately that by 'appreciating' your honesty, I didn't have to confront you about how rude and insulting it was to always feel like there was someone else you were more attracted to." I looked down, then continued quietly. "And if I'm really honest, maybe I didn't have to confront myself about why I was afraid to challenge you, or why I was doubting myself after almost twenty years of marriage."

Big exhales from both of us. I looked back into his eyes, afraid I might see anger, but only saw concern. And love.

"Anything else you need to say?" Reuel asked gently. I shook my head, drained.

"I just want you to know, so we can both hear it now together, that you are the only one I've wanted to be married to and to make love with. Yeah, I may find other women attractive at times, but it never goes beyond an appreciation. Like when we walk around Lake of the Isles. I appreciate the architecture and landscaping of those homes, and find many of them attractive, but I don't want to live there!" I smiled at that. "I'm committed to our home and to us," he reassured me.

Nearly two decades after our wedding, I risked confronting my doubts by unpeeling another layer for Reuel to know about me. I feared it would throw me into free fall, but instead, thanks to Reuel's willingness to know and value me, I landed in a gentle place.

8
Connecting

"Love rituals and intimacy rituals are like regular sex and special sex; the first is a familiar and reliable companion, the second you can get yourself prepared for but always feels like a gift."
—William J. Doherty

End of the First Week in December

Reuel has come through his first week-long inpatient chemo treatment not too worse for wear, considering all the horror stories people felt obligated to share. He seems to be rebounding well at home during this second week after treatment, feeling strong and even doing some dishes before I got home from work last night. Right now, he's looking at me with that familiar Friday-night gleam in his eye. I've always teased him that he could be on his deathbed and still waggle his eyebrows or give me that certain look that leaves no doubt about what he wants to be doing with me. We plan for two days out, Sunday afternoon, to make love.

The forces of nature seem to be working in our favor this time. The new snow and bitter cold discourage any drop-in visitors, create a beautiful view from the upstairs bedroom, and provide an excuse to use the fireplace to maximize the romantic mood. By now we are so ready to BE with each other I don't know whether to burst into flames or tears. One thing about getting a cancer diagnosis: it has the potential to propel you into living in the moment, which has wonderful payoffs for sexual encounters. Since the diagnosis, each love-making session has had its own intensity. This afternoon we feel the full range of intense attraction, intense sweetness, intense urgency, and intense intimacy. When we are finished, both of us drained and complete, I wonder aloud to Reuel how anyone could possibly stand that intensity every single time. "I could," he says, not bragging but simply stating his reality. I know it's true.

 Inside Look: Marriage and Family Therapist (MFT) Teaching Classroom, Mid-Career

"I'm not sure why we need to ask about their sex lives," the young evangelical student said. "If they aren't coming in for sex problems, then why should I ask them? Especially since I'm so inexperienced myself!"

This topic about working with couples who are having sexual problems always brings up discomfort for some students, and not just the young ones. I see some of the middle-aged students shifting in their chairs, eyes down on their tablets. I turn the question back to the class.

"What do you think? Why might this be an important part of the relationship to explore? Or can we just leave it to the couple to figure out on their own?" I don't have to wait long for responses.

"What if they're too embarrassed or shy to bring it up?"

"What if it's a problem for one, but they're afraid it will hurt the other to talk about it?"

"My wife and I went to marriage counseling, and our therapist never asked the first question about our sex lives. We later decided we were relieved but also felt kind of cheated."

"Great comments," I respond, "and all valid points. Many therapists are uncomfortable being direct about sex, which concerns me, because how, then, will a client feel comfortable? If we ask about how they deal with money, conflict, parenting, but omit questions about their sexual relationship, what kind of message does that send?

"Some of you have indicated you want to work in church settings, and that's where some of the most confusing messages about sex have been internalized by your clients. Traditionally, the church's message has been 'Don't touch. Don't think about it. Don't do it.' And then once you get to the wedding night, all those messages are supposed to suddenly disappear and you should proceed with abandon. What if the psyche doesn't switch that fast? You as the counselor may need to help them understand that process and help them find or re-engage their 'ignitions.'

"Finally, I will remind you what marriage therapist Dr. David Schnarch believes: that a couple's sexual relationship is a metaphor for their entire relationship."

Our history of lovemaking hadn't always been so simple. Both of us came into the marriage with distorted ideas about sex, although we thought they were "normal." Long conversations during our courtship clarified how important it was for each of us to be able to give ourselves—body, mind, and spirit—to each other in ways we'd never previously given or received. We agreed it was important to wait to have sex until after the wedding. We wanted to experience our "first time" together. Well, that, plus I was terror-stricken at the thought of getting pregnant before we were married. I wasn't sure I could hold up under our families' collective disappointment and shame. So in the Age of Aquarius, free love, and newly marketed birth-control pills, we were an island of relative innocence.

Innocent, however, is not a word that fit the way Reuel looked at me while we were courting—or during the whole of our marriage, for that matter, despite the doubts that pestered me when I saw him look at other women. And while I was shy, there was no mistaking my feelings when we could escape to the old piano house on campus. Those rendezvous in the deserted third-floor dormer were smoking hot. If we were having this much fun with our clothes on, we thought, just imagine. . . .

One week before our own wedding, we drove two hours to a rural town in central Washington to attend a friend's wedding. Reuel sang two songs, the wedding was lovely, and we were eager to get back on the road because time alone together was a scarce commodity. We wound along the twisting highway, up hop-covered hills and down into dust-bowl valleys strewn with blowing sagebrush. Reuel drove, and I sat as close to him as anatomically possible. In those days before seat belts, the proximity between driver and rider telegraphed the seriousness of their romance.

We had just traveled a straight patch of the highway and were about to curve into a long sloping hill when the sky around us began to change. Reuel eased off the gas pedal as the night sky lightened, thinking we were meeting an oncoming car that hadn't yet dimmed their headlights. We climbed to the crest of the hill but found no car. We started up the next hill, and the sky grew dramatically eerie with shades of green eeking through the black, the stars fading, and panels of light flashing without thunderstorms. The closer we crept to the crest of the hill, the more vivid the light, unlike anything we'd ever seen. It looked like we were climbing straight into heaven.

"Oh no!" I cried. "God is coming, and I haven't had sex."

We held our breath as we peaked that hill when suddenly, exploding before us on the panoramic night sky, was the most glorious display of heavenly lights. They shifted first one way, then another, pulsing first pink, then greenish, then soft yellow, like some kind of charged mood lighting moving across the night sky. After a few moments, assured that it was neither God nor aliens coming to claim us and that we might make it to our wedding night after all, we exhaled and sped to the top of the next hill to see how the colors and lights moved. This lasted for three or four hills before the lights faded back into the inky, starry sky. Neither of us had spoken during that time, not wanting to break the spell. It was our first aurora borealis, the northern lights, not to be experienced again in such spectacle and portent for another thirty years when we lay on the fresh sod surrounding our new house to watch the light show that was occurring right over our roof.

We received the northern lights show as a wedding gift and good omen for the honeymoon. Our wedding was everything we had hoped: trumpets, flutes, candles, Reuel singing to me a song he never again sang at anyone else's wedding, heartfelt vows, and a tear-filled congregation. We greeted the guests, stole conspiratorial glances of impatience, fed each other cake, finally got to change into our "going away" outfits, and ran through the rice-throwing crowd to the decorated car. According to western frontier tradition, the wedding party and friends chase the newlyweds around town, honking and generally interfering with the couple's progress to their honeymoon. Reuel had worked out an alternate plan with his best man, however, and we switched cars so the crowd followed Glen in the decoy car while we made a clever get-away. Our moment of triumph lasted only to the outskirts of town, when I realized I had left the birth-control pills behind. We snuck back into town, I grabbed the pills, and we made another clean get-away. Considering how fertile we turned out to be, it was a fortuitous return.

Once at the hotel, we had to grab a bite to eat before we could do anything. I excused myself early to go up to the room to change into my new chiffon negligee, nervous now about how I'd look. I washed my face because Reuel said he wanted just me, that it wasn't a night for makeup. I could hear him outside the bathroom door, bumping into things. Maybe he was nervous, too.

I don't remember how we got into bed that night. I know we paused repeatedly to adjust bodies, move my long hair out of the way, start, restart, and adjust again. Passion, for me, was curbed by discomfort. Reuel was patient and undistracted, always looking into my eyes (well, almost always) to let me know he loved me, wanted me. I was more caught up in the wonder of finally completing our love than the desire, tears rolling out the corners of my eyes, dripping into my ears. I could stand it now, if the world came to an end.

We had waited eons to experience love-making, to give each other our bodies. After several hours and numerous trips to the bathroom for me, Reuel was spent, temporarily satisfied, and quickly asleep. I looked into the dark room, trying to take it all in: the freedom to love, the lifelong commitment we'd just entered, the way my body felt different now. *Finally*, I thought, *we can be free to really know each other, to really be known by each other.*

So why did I feel so unsettled?

It was not to be the last time I shed tears because of sex, nor is sexual intimacy an uncommon problem. As so many couples have shared with me when they sought help with sexual problems, when it was good, it was very, very good. When it was bad, it was despairing. Reuel and I heard dozens of stories in our office from unhappy couples who all had variations on a theme in which an initial sexual hurt became embedded and infected with negativity. "She's cold, frigid," one partner would begin to think to himself, until that idea became so rehearsed in his mind that he developed a hair-trigger anger response. The other partner might believe, "He's selfish and just uses me," and then look for evidence to justify her withdrawal or accusations. What once made them feel so close had become a source of pain and separation.

In our marriage, Reuel's frequency indicator had a higher set point than mine. It was not his only way of connecting—he was not a "crotch-attached" male—but sex was much more than a physical release for him. He was very clear that lovemaking was also spiritual. For me, sex was more of a nice bonus, like a hot-fudge sundae—sensual, lovely to share, but not required in my daily diet. He didn't understand how I could be so different.

"How is it we can connect on so many different levels but be disconnected when it comes to making love?" he asked more than once.

"I don't *feel* disconnected," I replied, sometimes embarrassed, other times implying that he was the one with a problem. And for many years, he did take it on as his problem:

"Am I burdening you with my desire?"

"Am I not attractive to you?"

"Are you too tired from the kids or homework? Do I need to help you more?"

It was a repetitive cycle throughout much of our marriage: long periods of joyful, playful, erotic intimacy punctuated by piercingly painful encounters that leveled us. The pattern usually played out after the kids were asleep, we had our grown-up conversations, and it was time for bed. Reuel would wait for me to finish a project or finish reading my book, and I would somehow never get to a stopping point. I was absorbed and unaware until I registered the heavy sigh beside me or until he would abruptly roll away and turn his light out. Sometimes he spoke.

"I thought we had agreed we were making love tonight," in a tone that was annoyed, frustrated, dejected, or as the cycle repeated, hopeless.

That, then, was my cue to be confused, misunderstood, put-upon, ashamed, contrite, and genuinely bewildered. I loved Reuel. I knew he loved me. Why was I not as interested as he was? Was something wrong with my libido?

"Where does your sexual energy go?" he asked repeatedly, usually from curiosity. But as time went on and he saw no substantial changes in me, he asked out of anguish.

"Maybe I don't have as much as you do," I replied, trying not to sound as defensive as I felt.

"You are a sexual being. You have sexual energy. It's how we are wired. What do you do with your sexual energy? Where does it go? Would you please just notice that in yourself?"

Meanwhile, I was further into my graduate work, having moved into the phase of training that required me to take family-of-origin courses for my doctoral work in marriage and family therapy. My anxiety mounted when I realized I had to interview family members and ask questions that had been taboo in my family. The prospect of asking my dad how he learned about "the birds and the bees" sent shivers through me, way beyond just being uncomfortable. I realized I was going to need extra support, so decided to sign up for my own therapy. Doing so had been a tickle in the back of my mind for a while, at least in those moments when I wondered if Reuel's questions about my sexual energy had merit. Delving into my family of origin spread the focus beyond me. I invited Reuel to join me, and he didn't hesitate. *Humph, he doesn't have to be that eager*, I thought to myself. *I don't need that much therapy.*

I began talking with my family members, both close and distant, and then took the information to my therapist for us to sift through. It didn't take much excavation to discover that my family patterns were organized around one person—my father—who was the only one allowed to feel and behave in reactive ways. My mother, brother, and I rotated around him in our own characteristic ways, but it usually fell to me to soothe the angry beast and reduce the temperature in the household.

"Why did your father allow *you* to calm him?" Maude, my therapist, asked.

"He always liked me, even when he was fighting with me," I explained. My stomach began to sour as I went on. "I always made him look good."

"How do you mean?"

"Well, for example, when I was a child, people in elevators would stop and tell him what a pretty little girl I was. Diners at nearby tables in restaurants would come over and tell him how well-behaved and nicely mannered his daughter was. He beamed, as if he were totally responsible, the best dad in the world."

My stomach was churning as I blurted out, "I had to be who and how he wanted me to be. I had to reflect well on him so he could feel good about himself. I wasn't allowed to have my own opinions or my own style. It was only about what he wanted." I started to weep. Reuel handed me the box of tissues.

"Where was your mother with all of this?" Maude wanted to know.

"She came in second to me. Dad started turning to *me*, not my mom, for opinions. He considered *me*, not his wife. He held the door open for *me*, showed courtesies to *me* at the restaurant, asked what *my* preference was for the upcoming holiday."

Maude and Reuel were quiet as they saw me putting pieces together. I felt sure my dad had not sexually abused me, but why did I feel so icky?

"Even though my mom liked that I reflected well on her also, mostly she wanted me to be treated better by my dad than she was treated. And I was."

"And what's that like for you now?" Maude asked.

"It totally creeps me out," I gasped. Then the realization landed: I was in a spouse's role. I was my dad's wife. The creepiness kept building until it pushed out deep sobs.

When the session was over, I peeled myself off the couch, grabbed the hand Reuel extended, and wobbled out the door with his arm around me.

He and I continued to talk through the following days, as more pieces of my family jigsaw puzzle fell into place. The more I fit the puzzle pieces together, the more incensed I got. The slow burn grew to a boil one Saturday morning in the kitchen. I whipped around from the sink, eyes pinned on Reuel, who was innocently drinking coffee and reading the newspaper.

"Why weren't the rest of us allowed to have feelings about things?" I demanded.

"Uh . . ."

"Why were his needs the only ones that counted? Why was he more important than anyone else in the family? Why did we have to worry about his feelings?" Each question grew louder and more insistent. Understanding broke over Reuel's face, but I wasn't finished. "Didn't we have a right to be soothed and comforted? I was the child, for goodness' sake, not him!" Then the thought of my parents, particularly my father, comforting me sent shivers down my spine. I was repulsed.

Reuel waited to see if I was finished. He stood to refill his coffee as I abruptly sat on a kitchen chair. On his way back to the table, he squeezed my shoulder. I looked up at him with watery eyes.

"I'm sorry . . ." he ventured, offering the genuine soothing that was so infrequent in my childhood. I put my hand on his and nodded.

"Thanks." I thought a bit and began to work it out. "I think I have this tendency to want comfort but not be comfortable with it." It was a profound understanding for me. And now, looking back, I realize it must have taken great restraint on Reuel's part not to burst into the "Hallelujah" chorus. Instead, he ventured a few questions.

"Do you think that might account for the wall that pops up sometimes when we make love? Is that what you had to erect in order to protect yourself from the invasive narcissism of your dad?"

It was a good question and spot-on. Over the next several days, I realized that I didn't always recognize when the wall showed up. Typically, if Reuel mentioned it, I got defensive, then he backed off. But at some point during my therapy, maybe as he saw me change, Reuel changed. Suddenly he no longer backed off when I got defensive, much to my dismay. He wanted answers; I wanted avoidance. He wanted responses to his questions and concerns, not the status quo.

One morning, after a particularly painful sequence of my defensiveness and his discouragement, Reuel grew very clear.

"I want to get closer to you in every way, body, mind and spirit, but that damn wall has got to go. I'm willing to help you scale it or knock it down, but life is too short to ignore it and let it determine how close we're going to be."

He had put the ball in my court. Was I going to engage in this challenge to get closer, or was I going to run away? I didn't know how to answer him, but I realized I had grown weary of avoidance.

The next evening, the kids had all gone to bed, and we began to follow up on the signals we had made to each other earlier in the day that tonight might be the night. I showered, changed into a silky nightgown, and thought I was as ready as Reuel to be swept into sexual oblivion. We kissed, and our engines ignited as we moved onto the bed and felt passion building. Suddenly my feelings went as flat as a dial tone. The wall appeared. I was immobilized.

No! How could this happen? Why now? Can I ignore it? No, because Reuel sensed something amiss. I was kissing him, but he stopped and looked into my eyes. To my horror, I couldn't hold his gaze. The mood was broken. He pulled back and leaned against the headboard while I hung my head and scrunched into a mortified ball beside him. He was frustrated, and I was discouraged, both of us emotionally stretched to the point of tears. I thought that because I had decided I wanted to be close and stop my avoidance, I would be fine. But that wasn't enough to prevent the wall of disconnection from appearing. Was it always going to block me from being as close as I wanted? Would we ever be able to achieve the sexual intimacy we both desired?

I couldn't stand the thought of things continuing in this pattern. Something had to change! My despair gave me the courage to ask myself what I really wanted.

I wanted Reuel. I wanted intimacy. Then, with clarity, I saw my two competing terrors: that I would *not* experience that level of authenticity and transparency and that I *would* experience it. It was the ultimate intimacy dilemma.

By now I had slumped off the bed and was sobbing. Reuel, sensing a difference, joined me on the floor and put his arms around me. From somewhere deep within me, the word "shame" floated to consciousness. I started to dismiss it, then stopped. *Shame?* My head told me sex was not shameful, but my heart was consumed with shame. *Aaaagh, I feel shame about sex*, I realized. I felt scared to admit it to Reuel, but I knew I must open the lid on it. This brought a new round of crying. Finally, I spoke.

"I'm afraid," gasping between sobs, "that if I say what's really true—that I feel shameful about sex—you won't like me," I said, crying so hard into his shoulder I could barely breathe. I had spoken my shame.

Reuel held me tighter. He spoke tenderly, "Don't you know I'm crazy about you?"

His words of acceptance infused me. The crying stopped, my body calmed. Shame drained out of me and in its place was a peace so stunning I wondered fleetingly if it was real. He continued to hold me in simple love. When we finally climbed back into bed, we fell into an exhausted sleep.

9
Yielding

"Spouses must navigate the porcupine's dilemma—
the desire to achieve deep intimacy while remaining
invulnerable to pain."
—Eli Finkel

Second Week of December

*I'm hurriedly pouring coffee into a thermos before I leave the house
to meet clients. A scream howls down the stairwell, and I rush up to
see Reuel on the top two steps in the worse pain I've yet to witness—
his face contorted, his hands white from gripping the railing. He is
frozen on the steps, in so much pain he can't move, and I feel frozen
myself, seeing the pain written on his face. I grip his waist, he leans
on my shoulder and the handrail—dear God, what if I slip too?—and
we move down the stairs one excruciating step at a time.*

*Now we have to inch along the hall, elongated to a marathon
distance, as I grab coats and cell phones and anything else within
reach I think we may need for the day. Suddenly, we're seated in the
van—how did we get Reuel in here?—and I back out of the driveway
and tear down the highway, calling the doctor about whether to bring
Reuel to the office or the ER. He hears the uncharacteristic moaning*

from Reuel in the background and sends us to the hospital. I whip into the emergency entrance, run around the van to help Reuel out. I don't know if we need a wheelchair. I feel helpless and stunned. Thankfully, a maroon-coated volunteer materializes beside Reuel, who cannot bear to sit, and together we become human bolsters for his plodding journey to X-ray. The oncology office must have called ahead and cleared the way for us.

Evidently, he started down the stairs to the kitchen when one stocking foot slipped, and he brought his other leg down hard to catch himself. Something snapped. The films show his upper pelvic bone is fractured. Lymphoma, in its affinity for bone, has honeycombed its way through the top third of Reuel's pelvic region. So when he slipped on the steps, a fracture was inevitable. I'm deliberately not thinking about how unconstrained the lymphoma must be that his pelvis yielded so readily.

They hospitalize him to manage his pain levels, and we ride the patient elevator to the now-familiar oncology unit. The nurses and staff welcome us back, but these are the last people we want to see.

 Inside Look: Couples Counseling, Mid-Career

We knew we couldn't address the couple work between Laurie and Jessica until we addressed Jessica's trauma, so Laurie went to Reuel while Jessica and I worked together. Once her trauma was addressed, we arranged for all four of us to meet. We started with their recurring conflict over household chores.

"I work every bit as hard as Laurie," Jessica charges right in, "so why is it my job to make sure we have enough groceries, the bathrooms are clean, and the kids' backpacks are checked?"

"I do as much as you do. It just looks different. I may not clean the way you do, but I take care of household maintenance, which you don't!" Laurie leans forward, sporting a smug smile.

"Okay," I interrupt, figuring Reuel and I have heard all we need to get the gist of their argument. "It sounds like you're fighting over who has the right to say how things are going to be, like what's fair and what the standards are."

"And those kinds of conflicts," Reuel jumps into the discussion, "are almost always about power and control issues."

They both frown. "What do you mean?" Jessica asks. "We both believe we're equal, and we want to model that for our kids."

"I don't doubt that at all," Reuel responds, "but even in the most egalitarian couples, there are still power/control issues to work out."

"What makes you think that's what it's about?" Jessica's frown deepens as she and Laurie both fold their arms across their chests. *Uh-oh*, I think. *This is not going to be an easy sell.*

"Well, for one thing, the number of times you've told us you've had the same argument, because that means the problem isn't being fixed. See, if the issue is the issue, the issue can be resolved, but if the issue is power/control, you can be caught in a terminal power struggle."

Laurie sucks in her breath. "That sounds deadly!"

"Yeah," Reuel replies, "it sure can feel that way inside the relationship." He glances at me and smiles. "I mean, ahem, theoretically, of course, not from actual experience!" We all laugh at the welcome comic relief.

After we catch our breath, I come back with, "What might be helpful is to identify the core issue. Is the core issue that chores get accomplished? Is it that you are too exhausted, Jessica, and aren't caring for yourself? Laurie, are you afraid you would be giving something up by doing more daily chores? Each of you need to ask yourself what is keeping your own self—not your partner—stuck." They still look a little confused.

"Stuck places," Reuel explains, "suggest there's something you're not wanting to let go. It may seem like if you let go of power in this area, if you yield, then you would lose. The question is, what is it you would have yielded? What would you have lost? There's a big difference between losing the fight over who cleans the toilet and losing your relationship because you need to win every skirmish."

One of my favorite definitions of "giving," from Merriam-Webster, describes it as a "yielding of possession by way of exchange." We give something in exchange for receiving something, which could be as innocent as giving flowers to receive the look of joy on the recipient's face. On the other hand, giving could have ulterior motives, such as yielding a committee chair position in exchange for receiving the deciding vote for the direction of the corporation.

We usually think about yielding in terms of a loss, especially loss of power, not so much about what we might receive. Certainly, power and control issues are part of any relationship—family, work, religious, and especially partnered relationships. One of my mentors, James Maddock, always broached this topic by first defining "power" as the ability to influence and "control" as the ability to *limit* influence.

In my original family, my dad excelled at power plays while my mom mastered the art of control tactics. When he wanted something she didn't agree with, she knew just how long to ignore him until he was ready to yield some of his demands. She tended to run interference for my brother and me when Dad's demands were a bit too outrageous, but there was one time, right before Reuel and I were married, when I thought I could take Dad on myself.

My parents had set up a wedding gift display in the small balcony room of our apartment above the funeral home. I was checking the list of thank-you notes when my dad walked in. I don't remember how the exchange started, but he asked, in a complaining, critical voice, why I hadn't informed him about a particular wedding detail. I looked up from writing my thank you's and realized I had had enough of the usual power routine. Surprisingly bold, I chose to tell him the truth, which had been accumulating for nineteen years.

"Because I never know how you'll react. I don't know if you'll be mad, go along with it, or explode all over me." There! It was out! I don't know which of us was more shocked. The stunned silence quickly shifted to anxious silence until he began to gasp.

"Oh," he groaned. "If I thought you really believed that, I don't know what I would do."

I wasn't finished. "It's true. I never know which dad I'll get. I can't predict you."

"How could you say that?" He started to cry, only without tears. "I would be so hurt to have you think that. Here it is, a week before the wedding, and to think my daughter thinks of her daddy that way! I just don't know if I could stand it." His hand pressed against his heart.

Oh no. Not his heart. I refused to be responsible for his having a heart attack. It was an effective power move on his part, because he influenced me into backing way off. Truth was not a commodity that was valued in our household.

By then I was sobbing at my upset, at his distress, and, on some level, at the compromise or yielding I knew I would have to make. I ran to my bedroom, crumpled onto my bed, and cried prayers to God for deliverance and forgiveness. It never occurred to me that I was not obligated to fix my father's hurts. In our family, if dad was hurt then others' hurts were a distant second. After a few minutes, I gathered myself with deep breaths and went back. He stood just inside the doorway of the balcony room, neck stiff, but eyes down, covertly watching for me. He had known I would come back.

I spoke. "Uh . . . I didn't really mean what I said. It must have been these birth control pills I'm taking." Good, he twitched at that reference, so I knew he wouldn't ask more questions. "I'm sorry. Can you forgive me?"

His face transformed, and he smiled at me. "Of course. I just couldn't stand to think my Judy-bug felt that way about her daddy. But that's okay. You're going to have the best wedding."

My utter concession was complete. I had yielded my truth in exchange for my dream wedding and a semblance of family harmony. The lesson I absorbed and took into my marriage is that giving (yielding) meant losing a part of myself.

Reuel grew up with family power-and-control dynamics that looked different from mine but also impacted him in persistent ways. He came from parents whose memories of the Great Depression were so vivid that his mother saved the cardboard tubes from toilet paper rolls in case they'd be needed for a future craft project. That box of toilet paper tubes, along with a box of rocks for a future garden, were moved across the country several times before she was convinced to discard them. His father also was frightfully frugal, keeping track of long-distance phone calls—before cell phones, when an out-of-town call cost money—calculating who made which call to whom and billing each family member or houseguest down to the penny owed. His father's power over finances was indisputable (which Reuel absorbed and would later have to confront in our marriage), but his miserliness cost him. His lack of yielding generated a scarcity climate in the family and turned the members into survivors.

As a result, Reuel learned to not ask for things in order to protect himself from disappointment. When he graduated high school, however, he thought his parents might alter their pattern, so he ventured a special request. He had spotted a Grundig radio in one of the local shops and risked presenting his case since music was also soul-soothing to his mother.

"Mom, this is one of the best-made radios out there. It

has quality you can't get on any of the transistors, it's made in Germany, and they last forever. I can take it with me to college and have music in my room," he argued, knowing his mother always supported his music. "I know it's $87, but most of the other parents in the church are spending around $200 on the graduation gift." His mother looked receptive and even went with him to see the radio and listen to the sound. He was hopeful.

When graduation came, he opened the card from his parents to find a check for $25. The small opening in his heart that would allow him to ask for things slammed shut. He quit wanting things. What he learned and took into our marriage was that asking created vulnerability. To ask for something, even to authentically receive a gift, meant he had to yield his protection.

✉

In the case of our marriage, giving through yielding broke new ground within each of us. Initially we yielded our most private views of life, the parts of ourselves that hadn't yet seen the light of day, and offered them to each other. We presented to one another that part of ourselves that made us feel most like an outsider, and by yielding it and receiving from each other, we found a kindred spirit. That assurance of kindred spirits helped embolden us when we reached inevitable power-and-control struggles, whether they were over finances, sex, or life-and-death decisions.

And it did require boldness! Such mutual exchange exacted different efforts from each of us. I had to bypass my default drive to seal myself up in order to yield glimpses into the authentic me. I had to work at letting myself out. Reuel had to bypass his default drive to protect himself by yielding his boundary and letting another's influence enter. He had to work at receiving. We each needed to yield, but in different directions: I needed to give more of myself to Reuel, and he needed to let more of my love in.

Reuel didn't realize the extent of just how difficult it was to receive from me until we were about thirty years into our marriage. What started out to be a fun experience suddenly showed him how challenged he still was to receive. We had just picked out granite countertops for the kitchen, which for rock-loving Reuel meant that he was the proverbial kid in a candy store. After the counters were installed, I would sometimes come around the corner to find Reuel, flashlight in hand, 6'4" frame stretched out over a length of the counter, eagerly looking into the depths of the rock. I was delighted with his pure enjoyment and one day expressed as much to him. Later that night, he said he'd been reflecting and wanted to talk. Immediately my defenses shot up.

"This morning, when we talked about the granite and how you knew I've always liked rock and granite, you went on to talk about how happy you were for me to get some granite that is really nice."

"Yeah . . ." I wasn't sure where this was going.

"Well, I heard your words of happiness for me, and maybe I said thanks. But at the same time, I had the ever-so-fleeting sense of your words going into me about an eighth of an inch, then bouncing off. It was one of the first instances I've experienced that in real time."

I felt such relief at hearing that he finally understood

this, I almost jumped up and clapped, but he looked so vulnerable with his head bowed that I wanted to proceed with caution. "That sounds big . . ." Not a brilliant response, but his eyes came back to mine.

"This is really hard to name, but I realized that just the act of acknowledging to myself—let alone you—how something of such beauty touches me. . . . Well, it instinctively felt risky and vulnerable." His voice began to break. I reached a hand to him.

"Why vulnerable?" I asked.

"Well, I believed I was supposed to experience being touched by beauty, but not let anyone know, because then I wouldn't be hurt. The power of the beauty I felt about the granite was immense, but I wasn't supposed to say anything. When I did say something, you were not only supportive but happy for me and told me how much you wanted it for me."

"Uh, was that the wrong thing?" My frown lines must have been deepening in my confusion.

"Oh, no! It was a beautiful thing to say, but deep down I believe I'm not supposed to have other people wanting something for me as much as I want it for myself. You weren't even supposed to see what I wanted, let alone remember it and then want it for me."

His face began to crumble in slow motion, tears building in his eyes, but he wasn't finished. "I remembered, then, that this is what you've referred to in the past."

"How so?" I hoped my tone was soothing as my heart went out to him.

"Those times when you expressed genuine love for me, and I didn't 'get it' or let it in." The tears began to spill from

94

his eyes then. "That was painful to accept, but I see it's true. I'm sorry for those times, and I wish I could have begun to let it in sooner."

I jumped up to hug him and we embraced for several moments, but he wasn't quite finished. He reached into his pocket, pulled out a small slip of paper, and gave it to me.

"These words are as much for me as for you," he explained. I opened the note:

I am trying to do it differently now and will continue to let your love soak more deeply into those places that have been too scary to let anyone into. I love you very much—thank you for the gift of your love.

I wasn't trying, at least in this instance, to exert power over Reuel to open up and let my love influence him. It was a much more intimately powerful, organic experience for him to—on his own—yield his control or protection in exchange for a deeper-felt experience of love.

10
Bonds

"Loving deeply means that we must enter the world
of the other person and come to understand them from the inside
out in a soul-to-soul encounter."
—Chelsea Wakefield

Mid-December

*The pain from Reuel's hairline pelvic fracture is under control,
and he is back home and getting around surprisingly well. He does
some chores around the house, rests a bit, then does a few more. My
thoughts turn with relief toward the impending holidays. I want
something in our lives to be normal.*

*As I put away dishes, I'm aware of Reuel's silence, which
usually means he has been mulling over something. A few minutes
later, he asks me to take notes for him, because he feels the need to go
into the Flow. I want to be supportive, so I brighten my face and say,
"Great!"*

*My stomach clenches a bit, wondering if he's as uneasy as
I am that we have yet to see progress in his condition. The doctors
have not found a chemical cocktail that will halt the lymphoma. How
many more of these intensive in-patient chemotherapy treatments*

can his body withstand?

At this point in his treatment, the stakes are so high that it's all I can do to keep from telling Reuel to ask for an instant healing when he goes into the Flow. How many more disappointments can our kids and I tolerate? It seems to me it would be much better for him to just be instantly healed. I don't want to express my doubts to Reuel right now. He looks so vulnerable, with his bald head and sagging posture.

We trudge up the stairs to the bedroom and assume our positions — he at the footboard, me at the headboard — facing each other on the king-sized bed. It has become our prayer rug, our altar, at these times. I am poised with pen and tablet. He opens his prayer conversation with the Divine by expressing his sense of fear and paralysis:

"The path seems too difficult right now. I'm trying to hold onto words, messages, trust, divine whispers, and assurances in the spiritual part of me. But I'm finding it hard to reconcile with the physical part. I'm scared I'll always be in pain and that I'll die anyway. I'm afraid of abandoning Judy and the kids by dying, afraid of the grief and pain they would go through by losing me and forcing Judy to find someone else." His face is screwed up with imagining it.

"I just wanted to spare my family grief, and now I'm the source of it," he sobs and gasps, "and there's nothing I can do about it. It's beyond my control, which is a good thing, probably . . . I experienced too much grief growing up. I can barely stand the thought of making my family go through that. It would be my fault to cause this.

'It's not your fault.'" Reuel's voice is strong as he conveys this.

"When I hear your Voice say that, I want to trust it. Most of

all, I want strength.

'Trust is stronger than death.'

"*I am surprised to hear that. Death seems stronger than trust. The fear of death seems stronger than trust.*

'I am that I am. And because of that, things will be.'

"*My pain is understood. It's just about trust. So the presence of pain and fear seems to be outweighing trust. It doesn't nullify it. It will just be what it will be. Nothing is forever . . ." Reuel says, shaking his head no.*

'Is there anything more that you want to know?'

"*I want to know all, and I want to know nothing.*

'The question is the same for you, Judy.'"

Gulp. I'm in the Flow now, too. My mind races. "Is trust the same as wisdom?"

"*'One is part of the other. Wisdom can come from years. Trust comes from the Divine. Wisdom can also come from inside a person, but this kind of knowing comes from the Divine. At times, trust, knowledge, and wisdom are the same—like the Trinity of Father, Son, and Holy Spirit. But there is still a wisdom that can come from years, if you allow it. Fear can make these things difficult, but not insurmountable. I understand the struggle of fear and trust coexisting. Everything is known, and nothing is new. Nothing has changed. It will be what has been decided.'*

"*That seems to be the end of that," Reuel concludes. "It just simply will be."*

✉

We blink our eyes and come back into ourselves.

Later that evening, Reuel and I are still processing the power-

ful experience. He asks me to do more note-taking for him.

"This time," he explains, "it's more like a journal entry instead of prayer."

It is an unusual request from him. He typically learns through listening and then talking. He has rarely used journals. Of course I will record his thoughts—note taking is my thing! That's how I best learn. We don't go up to the bedroom this time. Instead, he expands himself into "The Bahamas," what he named the recliner. ("I can't stand the thought of being bound to a recliner," he once stated, "but I don't mind spending time in the Bahamas.") I get a pen and paper and a cup of tea. When I get settled on the leather couch beside him, he closes his eyes and begins to speak.

"My greatest fear now, the most raw place, is the thought of dying and leaving you. Because I believe our relationship is special beyond the average relationship, it seems inconceivable that the bond would be broken before its time. Breaking that bond," he sobs, "is worse, more painful than the fear of my own death. Every time I've had that thought, I've brushed it aside. It's too raw and painful to contemplate. It just seems inconceivable. That's my greatest fear and pain. It's beyond the physical. I'm afraid to say it, afraid to admit it to you and to me. But now it's been said."

He opens his eyes and looks at me, tears spilling over his cheeks. I am sobbing, torn between wanting to comfort him and wanting to curl up from the raw pain. I manage to move and collapse onto Reuel in the recliner. He holds me tightly. Soon his shirt is wet from my tears, and my hair is damp from his.

Much later, I realized that Reuel wanted me to journal his thoughts because, as he told me later, putting it on paper "made it all the more real and true." I wondered if he was trying to prepare me in some way, if he had a sense of what was to come. Perhaps he wanted me to comprehend something in the way I best learned. But it was too raw and painful for me to contemplate except in flitting moments. It *was* inconceivable to imagine our bond broken by death.

11
Christmas

"Even those of us who are the helpers have to have help. That's the secret that's not often shared. Good helpers need helpers."
—Courtney Butler-Robinson

Fourth Week of December

It's two days before Christmas. Reuel is looking forward to Cory flying in from New York for the holiday. Aaron is under contract to a cruise ship in Hawaii, and our mothers are not well enough to travel from Washington or Indiana, so it will be a cozy Christmas with just Marci, Cory, and one of their friends. I'm feeling smug that we got the house decorated before the inpatient chemo started, back when Reuel felt well and strong enough to lug boxes up from the basement. Was that only a month ago? Time passes in dog years when he's in the hospital. He has another admission scheduled for the day after Christmas, but I'm not going to think about that right now.

Reuel settles into The Bahamas. I check to see if he needs any-thing before I leave to pick up Cory at the airport.

"Life is good in The Bahamas," he declares as I scan the scene. Medications are lined up on the end table beside him, a full glass of water awaits, the latest wine magazine lies on his lap, and a hand-

made comforter is tucked around his legs. I start to load his favorite
Christmas CDs into the player, but he stops me.

"Don't put the Martins' CD in."

I jerk my head around in surprise. The brother-and-sisters
trio is one of his favorites.

"What?" I ask and see his eyes are moist.

"I don't think I can handle that right now. You know how
their 'O Come, O Come Emmanuel' moves me every year, even when
I'm feeling my best." He blinks a few times. "This year it's just too
close."

"Okay." I'm struck by his request. He usually maintains such
an upbeat attitude that this moment of vulnerability around music—
his usual source of strength—gives me pause. My mind starts to
wander to the cliff's edge of "What if?" and I quickly rein it in. No, I
refuse to tailspin right now. It's Christmas. *I take slower breaths,*
backing away from the thought.

I put the Martins' CD back in the case and load the others.
It'll be so nice to have our regular Christmas next year, *I think.*
And we'll look back at this year wondering how we did it
and be grateful that we got our lives back. We just have to get
through this next chemo round.

I head to the airport. It's a typical Minnesota December day,
with low clouds so engorged they look like they'll pop with snow glit-
ter. We haven't seen Cory since last summer, when he shaved Reuel's
head after the first chemo treatment. I stop the car by the curb, get
the call that he's picked up his bag, and then we see each other with
cell phones to our ears. Our curly-headed, Hollywood-ready son runs
over, drops his bag, and enfolds me in a big hug.

Suddenly I'm crying against his chest, not just a few tears
slipping out but deep, silent sobs that come so fast I can hardly catch

my breath. I'm as surprised as Cory at the depth of my emotion, and he starts sniffling too. As the tears subside, we get into the car to drive home.

"Wow, I didn't expect that," I say, wondering if being with Cory gave me safety to let out my pent-up feelings.

"Yeah." He chuckles a bit. "I knew you missed me, Mom, but really . . ." We laugh. Then he asks, "Are you okay? Is Dad okay?"

"Well, I'm okay. I guess everything just snuck up on me." I'm less sure how to answer about his dad. This is the kid who feels his emotions mostly in his stomach. He's not been calling us as often as he used to, and I know it's because he's afraid of what he might hear. I decide to start with the basics and see how he responds.

"Dad is hanging in there. He's been in lots of pain, so he can be pretty out of it from the narcotics. He's really glad you're here."

"I'm really glad I'm here, too." He responds with certainty, but he asks nothing else. I realize that's as much as he needs for now. I might have to titrate the information in small doses so his system can get used to this new reality.

When we arrive home, Cory takes his bag into the house, spots his father, and takes giant strides across the room to hug him. Reuel shuffles in the recliner, trying to stand, but Cory moves in before he can get up. He insists on standing, and Cory helps him. I hold my breath, wondering about Reuel's pain level. With tears, they embrace in a bear hug. I am stunned to see that Cory, who used to be three inches shorter than his dad, is now the same height. This can't be good, I think. Reuel is shrinking. No! I'm not going to think about that now, either. The knot in my stomach loosens. I have Christmas to get ready for, after all.

Christmas Eve. All the candles are lit, the music plays in the

*background, the fire purrs in the fireplace. We all soak in the beau-
ty of the room, feeling the mystery and magic that make this night
special every year. But this time it's different. I catch myself staring,
trying to absorb the warmth of each person, and I see Reuel, Cory,
Marci, and her friend Dawn doing the same. We smile at each other
often. Then we quickly look elsewhere, unable to hold eye contact for
long. It hits me how intensely intimate this evening is. It is spiritual
in a way that goes beyond a typical Christmas Eve service or the family Christmas carols we usually send soaring into the vaulted ceiling.
A deeply satisfying warmth spreads through my chest.*

*The next morning, when it is time to open gifts, Reuel is fog-
gy from pain medication, but he makes a concerted effort to hand me
one particular gift. I raise an eyebrow. "When and how did you get
this?" I ask, remembering our agreement to keep it a low-key Christmas.*

*"I still have a few tricks up my sleeve," he says, a dull twinkle
in his eyes. His note on the gift card looks like the handwriting of his
father at ninety-two years, but he has packed love into the few words.
And a mystery, because the note says, "This is only part one of the
gift." I look over at him again, questioning. "You'll just have to wait
and see," he says.*

*I open the small present and gasp. He has always been the
best giver of jewelry, but this time the box holds one-hundred-fifty-
watt diamond earrings. I'm shocked and delighted.* Where and how
did he get them?

*"Well, you said you might want some bling." He smiles. I
put them on immediately. Marci takes a picture of me pointing to my
ears, and they all chant, "She's got bling!"*

*Reuel looks exhausted from his brief effort, but he continues
to give and receive with as much presence as he can muster. His eyes*

fill with tears frequently, which then brings tears to us, as we share our hearts and presence with each other. The presents are a bonus. Periodically, reminders of the looming hospitalization that will come the next day intrude into my awareness. I'm getting pretty good at shoving them aside.

Inside Look: Consultation Group, Early Career

"Judy, how's it going in your practice?" asked Noel. She had supervised me for the requirements for my psychology and MFT licensure, but I enjoyed her wisdom and our group members so much that I wanted to continue in the group.

"It's so interesting . . . You know how we've talked in the past that certain client issues appear in your practice like waves? First you get a wave of couples fighting over money, then a wave of couples where someone is having an affair? Well, now I have a wave where one of the partners has cancer."

"And how are they handling it?" she asked.

"In the first couple, the husband carries the diagnosis. It's his second marriage, and his four adult daughters have been totally estranged from him up until he left a message for them about his cancer. Now they are super concerned, calling him, asking if they can stop by, but it's all a bit unsettling to the new wife, who hasn't been used to sharing him."

"What about the other couple?" asked Steve, another group member.

"In this one, the wife was recently diagnosed. They have three little kids, and the husband has evidently freaked out. He won't come with her to therapy, and she describes how he spends most of the day at work or somewhere else, only coming home to catch a few hours of sleep and change clothes. She feels abandoned by him at a time she and the kids most need him. In fact, she thinks he's having an affair."

We were all quiet for a few moments, then Noel responded. "Those are striking examples of the extreme ways cancer can impact the family. In the first family you described, the father's cancer activated the alienated daughters to reunite them. The diagnosis became a bonding agent to hold them together, even though the new wife has to make room for the daughters.

"In the second family," she went on, "the wife's cancer may have revealed the hairline cracks in their marriage. With the burden of such a diagnosis, the brittle marriage couldn't contain the extra pressure, and you may be witnessing it shattering in slow motion." She looked at each of us in the circle in her office. "Cancer impacts families in extreme ways."

Then she focused her gaze on me. "Judy, you have some personal history with this, don't you?"

....

Eight years into our marriage, we were living in the Washington, D.C., suburbs, just inside the Maryland border, where Reuel pastored a small-but-loving church. Life was beginning to settle into the new normal, with three children in four years. I had just had my twenty-eighth birthday, had just ventured back to my first Sunday service after the new baby, when I felt a tap on my shoulder after the final "Amen."

I turned to see the man behind me, a dentist whom I'd earlier greeted.

"Have you ever experienced any thyroid problems?" he asked.

Huh? Could a question be any more random?

He continued before I could respond. "I'm asking because I noticed that you have an enlargement on the front of your neck. Had you noticed?"

Well, no. No I hadn't. My hand flew to the spot he was pointing to.

"Oh." I felt the lump, redness creeping up my face.

"You may want to get that checked out," he said. "It looks like it's in the area of the thyroid."

I dashed to the nursery, gathered up the babies, and rushed across the parking lot to the parsonage. After I got the kids settled, I dashed to the big wall-mirror in the living room. *Oh my gosh, look at that thing on my neck!* One side was swollen and bulging way out beyond the other side. How long had it been that way? How could I have not seen it before now? How could Reuel have missed it? He never missed anything.

When he came home, I described my exchange with the dentist, ending with a hand flourish to my neck in dramatic "Ta-dah!" fashion. I expected him to smile at my theatrics, but instead his face sobered.

"You better call the doctor right away," he said.

I was a little annoyed at his lack of humor. "I have my six-week OB checkup tomorrow, so I'm sure they'll take care of it then."

Thus started the parade of medical appointments, referrals to specialists, and inconclusive procedures. The standard diagnostic tests were forbidden because I was breastfeeding. At each consultation and procedure we were told, "The odds are small that it's anything to worry about . . ." Yet at each step, we'd been on the wrong side of the odds. With each appointment, the possibility of a life-threatening illness increased. We juddered from one meeting to the next, Reuel often more jolted than me.

We finally ended up in an endocrinologist's office, who decided a needle biopsy was indicated. By then it was the day before Christmas, the sky gray and oppressive. My parents had arrived to celebrate the holidays with their grandkids, only to learn something was wrong with their daughter. Their anxiety was so thick it was almost a relief when Reuel and I escaped to go to Georgetown University Medical Center for the needle biopsy.

We held hands and walked down corridors deserted for the holiday break, our footsteps echoing through the empty halls. My chest grew tighter the farther we plodded, and I had trouble catching my breath. It felt like the institutional equivalent of a gangplank. Finally, we spotted the lab.

The specialist herself greeted us and directed me to a wooden pew-like bench against the wall to examine the growth on my neck, gently turning my shoulders first one way then another to catch the best light. Finally, she spoke.

"Mrs. Tiesel, I am going to insert a long needle into this growth on your neck in order to capture some of the cells. I may have to do that two or three times to get a sufficient sample. Then, because it is Christmas Eve, I am going to take the cell samples to my lab to study them now. I want you to wait here so that I can give you a preliminary report." She waited for us to nod our agreement.

Of course I nodded. I always nodded. The doctor left briefly, but returned with a tray holding a foot-long cylinder that was more pipette than needle. *THAT is what gets injected into my neck?* Reuel's eyes expressed the same thoughts. I gripped Reuel's hand while she instructed me in the precise angle of my neck, the focus point to lock my eyes onto, and when to hold my breath amidst sensations of squeezing, pricking, and pressure. When she finished, she instructed us to wait while she made a preliminary reading under the microscope.

Reuel stood. I sat. He walked around the room. I sat and watched him. He stretched his hamstrings. I wiggled my toes. He bounced on his toes like he was at the free-throw line. I watched the clock. He sat beside me. I stood up. My legs shook, and I sat. *Long waits are never good news.* We planned what to do when we got home, counted how many presents were ready. I watched the clock. I started using my childbirth breathing exercises from three months earlier to quiet my uneasiness. *What is happening in that lab? Maybe I don't want to know. Maybe we'll just run down the halls, head back into the subway, and come back after Christmas.*

Then the doctor appeared.

"Because it's Christmas, I wanted to give you some kind of news so you wouldn't be worrying over the next few days. The cells suggest it's not just a cyst. It's not clear exactly what it is, but what I can tell you is that it is not the fastest growing kind of cancer. I wanted to relieve your minds with that news."

Suddenly I was up in the corner of the ceiling, looking down on the three of us, wondering when the relief would come. Reuel clenched my hand tighter, and I returned to my body, which was still holding its breath. I silently exhaled the word "cancer." My mind began to re-engage. Not the fastest growing kind of cancer, okay, but how many kinds are there—slow growing, medium growing, medium-fast growing, lightning speed? The doctor said she would send the results to my endocrinologist for the next step.

"At least it isn't the fastest growing kind of cancer," became my new mantra. We repeated it to each other and to my parents once we got home, although my father didn't seem to hear it. His style of coping with anxiety was to hand it off to someone else, but this time he had no takers. We each were already occupied with trying to manage our own fears. He looked at me as if I were "Dead Woman Walking," and it was all we could do to not get sucked into the black hole he was creating.

Cancer in a family may be like how Michelle Obama described the presidency: it "doesn't change who you are, it reveals who you are." Hit with the potentially deadly unknown, we suddenly were thrust through an existential looking glass and confronted with questions about who we really were. I began to ask the first of many questions:

Who am I if I don't take on and appease my father's anxiety like I've always done?

Who am I as a twenty-eight-year-old woman who may have just received a short life sentence?

Who is Reuel if he becomes a widower with three kids? Whom will he choose to marry next, and how will he keep my memory alive for our kids?

Who are we as spouses with three children under four?

Which relationship now takes priority — the marriage, the parenting, or trying to hang onto my own self in the midst of my newly shot-to-smithereens world?

Within a year, I would discover there were even tougher and more revealing questions to answer about myself and my marriage.

12
Standing Firm

"Being intimate with your partner doesn't mean you get the response you want . . . . Intimacy is not designed to make you feel one particular way; it's designed to make you grow."
—David Schnarch

First Week of January

We have now ticked off another round of intensive, inpatient chemo after Christmas and into this New Year, hopeful again that this latest is the one that will kick in and destroy the cancer. After the initial physical slump following each treatment, Reuel rallies in strength and stamina, although in my unguarded moments I realize his complexion is beginning to yellow, and he isn't bouncing back to baseline.

The therapist in me knows a blanket denial of the possibility of his dying is not healthy, so I let myself realize the gravity of going through three—or is it four?—different chemotherapy concoctions with zero impact on the lymphoma. The realization is a knife-blade of knowledge and fear that punctures my heart.

Stop. That's enough. I know it's serious. I've known from those first indicting X-rays that this was a deadly battle. But both Reuel and I are fierce warriors, and together we are always unbeatable.

This is just taking longer than we thought, but the lymphoma simply must succumb to the strength of our spirits. I remind myself of the number of people around the world who've told us they're praying for Reuel in private personal devotions, in sanctuaries and synagogues and temples. My fear begins to dissolve as I visualize a warm prayer infusion seeping into the cells of my body, pushing away the fear. I let my breath out. It's time to check on Reuel.

He's back in The Bahamas, his legs elevated after the latest complication of a blood clot that resulted from his immobilization after the pelvic fracture. The arsenal of pain relievers, antiemetics, hemoglobin boosters, and miscellaneous medications lined up for quick access each day could stock a small pharmacy.

"How ya doin'?" I ask.

"Doing okay," he responds in our verbal shorthand. "What's on your docket for today?"

"I've got a pretty full day of clients," I answer, glancing at my watch, "but I'll have my phone with me at all times, so don't hesitate to call."

"I won't. Hey, how is that one case going?" he asks, referring to a client situation I've consulted with him about.

"They might actually be making some progress," I say. "In fact, they're coming in today, so I'll let you know." I know that he really misses doing therapy, so I ask when he's planning to go back into the office.

"I think I can schedule a couple of clients next week if this pain from the blood clot keeps improving."

As I pack my day's supplies into the van, I'm aware that two constant forces are at work. One is the presence of the Divine, either in Spirit or through the support of friends. The other is the presence of pain in Reuel's body and its increasing demands.

Inside Look: Counseling Office, Later Career

"Oh, Dr. Tiesel, I feel so much better now that Paul and I are finally here to get marriage counseling. I just know things are going to be okay now," enthused Maggie, one half of the new client couple.

I look at Paul, who is staring at the floor. He doesn't appear to be feeling better. Time for me to give them my version of informed consent.

"I'm glad you're both here. Just calling and getting through the door that first time shows tremendous courage and a desire to be done with the status quo, the same old, same old of your marriage. But I may have some bad news for you."

Paul shoots his head up to make eye contact. Maggie pushes back farther into her chair.

"Working on your marriage is some of the hardest work you'll ever do, because it means that sooner or later, you will be working on yourself: how you feel, how you react, and who you want to be. It's hard because you can't just look at your spouse and complain about her or him. Instead, you need to ask yourself what your criticism about them means about you as a person."

"So then why are we here together, if we have to work on ourselves?" Paul challenges, and Maggie nods.

"I'm glad you asked! It's because we don't always know what to examine in ourselves if we're by ourselves. The stuff we most need to work on comes out in our relationships. That's both the good news and the bad news." Their silence indicated they were both taking in that information.

"Two other things I need to tell you. First, there will be times when you will think that I'm taking your spouse's side, that I'm unfair. You will be right! If my job is to help your marriage, then I may have to lean on one of you at one time to help balance the marriage, and then another time I may have to lean on the other. It's a kind of ratcheting effect where one of you may be the focus in order to move the marriage, and then the other one will be in the 'hot seat.' The goal is always the health of the marriage, which means that you as an individual have to contribute from a healthy place within yourself.

"Second, after hearing all of this, you may not be surprised to learn of my warning: You are going to feel worse before the marriage gets better."

....

When, almost three decades earlier, the discovery was made that I had a growth on my thyroid gland, the endocrinologist determined it needed to be removed (even though it wasn't the fastest metastasizing cancer). He referred me to a surgeon, who set a surgery date three weeks away. I needed at least that much time to wean the baby onto a bottle and make arrangements for childcare while I was hospitalized. Reuel's folks would come stay with him and the kids, and church members signed up to supply meals.

Meanwhile, Reuel had a bad feeling about this tumor. Privately, he knew—even felt confirmation from God—that the diagnosis was going to be cancer, but that it was going to be okay. Reuel didn't share that conviction with me, but in the three weeks before the surgery, he was withdrawn and preoccupied. Several times a day I called, "Reuel!" trying to flag his attention. Then he shook his head and asked me to repeat what I'd just said. I attributed his absent-mindedness to worry about losing me, and frankly, thought he was overreacting. I didn't realize he was carrying the burden of "knowing" the thyroid tumor was cancerous.

My own disquiet was channeled into preparations for the children and incoming grandparents. When the anxiety broke through all my busy work, yanking my attention with a hammering heart, I remembered that the needle-biopsy doctor told me it wasn't the fastest-growing kind of cancer. Then I could go back to the immediate focus of making and freezing casseroles or creating schedules for the grandparents while I was in the hospital.

Soon enough, the day of surgery came. Reuel and a few friends from the church sat vigil in the waiting room until the surgeon emerged with the results.

"It went well, your wife is doing fine, and we didn't have to remove the whole thyroid," the surgeon explained to Reuel (which he later reported to me).

"That means the frozen section was negative?" he asked.

"Yes, the frozen biopsy showed no signs of cancer, so we left the right half of the thyroid intact. We send all thyroid tissue to the labs, so we'll be getting the final path report back in about a week."

Reuel was relieved, but not jubilant. The quick, initial report in the operating room looked clear, but we hadn't gotten the final, more thorough, diagnosis. His earlier sense that the tumor was cancerous—but I would be okay—had not changed.

When we went to the surgeon's office for a post-op check, he delivered the results of the final path report about the thyroid tumor.

"Unfortunately, it is cancer," he reported in that no-affect medical voice. "We now need to decide what to do with the remaining half-thyroid you have."

My heart dropped to the pit of my stomach. I looked at Reuel; he didn't appear shocked.

The surgeon explained that the remaining thyroid gland was now a susceptible field for collateral cancer damage. Because the thyroid gland captures any iodine in the body, the medical team wanted to burn out the remaining thyroid with radioactive iodine so any remaining cancer no longer had a "home." A date was soon set.

We grabbed hands as we left the office, desperate to keep touching and not let go. Later, I would realize how different the looping messages playing in our heads were:

Me: *I'm only twenty-eight. I have three babies. I want to help them grow to adulthood. Were we too happy? Am I going to waste away and be out of my mind with pain? . . . I'm only twenty-eight. I have three babies . . .*

Reuel: *This is somehow my fault . . . Bad things happen to me . . . I always lose the ones I love . . . I should have done something different to prevent this . . . I'm the one who should die, not Judy . . . This is somehow my fault . . .*

Despite the inner demons we each were fighting, we

agreed that this next procedure was the correct one. Two weeks later, united in determination, we marched into the nuclear medicine department at George Washington University Medical Center. I was ushered into what looked like a study room in a library, instructed to sit at a desk, and draped in a lead apron. I waited a few minutes before doors swung open, and the nuclear-medicine specialist, taking slow, wedding-march strides, entered the room, arms extended in front of him, watching the lead-lined canister he carried. He set it on the desk in front of me.

"Don't touch it!" he warned as I jumped. I buried my hands more firmly in my lap.

In slow motion, he opened the lever on the top of the canister to reveal a glass cylinder, which he gradually raised from the lead casing. He then put a glass straw into the cylinder. This was one of the most solemn rites I'd ever witnessed, so I reacted like a nervous adolescent in church. I got the giggles. *Holy Radioactive Cocktail, Batman!* More giggles. He shot disapproving looks at me. *All this scene needs is a drum roll*, I thought, clamping my lips and swallowing my nervous amusement.

"Mrs. Tiesel, I'm going to hold this for you while you drink the contents through the straw."

I reached for it.

"Don't touch! And whatever you do, don't spill!"

As the weeks passed without further medical problems, our fears eased, and life once again settled into a routine with preschool, church activities, a hyperactive washing machine, and a second job for Reuel. We were really poor. We were really tired. We were really in love.

Soon, another year had passed, and it was time for the one-year follow-up scan of my thyroid to see if there had been any metastasis of the cancer. On the appointed day, Reuel delivered me into the nuclear medicine department where I was instructed to lie still for about an hour as a huge metal disc passed over my body. Afterward, in an all-too-familiar waiting room (don't they all look alike?), we waited for the results.

"There is tissue in your thyroid bed that should not be there," the specialist said. "We don't know if it is stubborn thyroid tissue that was not irradiated last year or if it is metastasized cancerous material."

"Then do I need another surgery to remove it?"

"No, the material is microscopic, and the surgeon would have difficulty seeing it and getting it all. After consultation with your doctors, we think you should have more radioactive iodine—a higher dose this time, since it will take a stronger measure to irradiate the stubborn tissue."

That didn't sound so bad. I just had to suck more liquid out of the lead-lined canister.

"What are the risks with this?" Reuel asked.

"Well, radiation is cumulative in the body. The risk is that it increases her chances of leukemia, a blood disease, by seventy-five- to a hundred-fold."

Stunned silence. Then Reuel erupted. "No! That's not acceptable."

The doctor and I exchanged glances, then I looked at the floor. I was more stunned at Reuel's response to the risk than to the news itself. Or maybe that was easier to focus on. I didn't know what to say, how to smooth over the tension in the room.

"You're telling me I have to sign a consent for my wife's radiation treatment that almost guarantees her chances of getting leukemia?" Reuel had never previously balked at signing the then-required spousal consent form for any of my other medical procedures.

"It is the best treatment for this type of cancer," the doctor explained.

"That's like signing her death warrant! I will not. There have to be other alternatives."

Warily, the specialist encouraged us to think about it and consult with others.

The ride home veered from cold to hot: chilly silence punctuated by heated arguments.

"The doctors obviously know more about this than we do. Why shouldn't we take their recommendations?" I huffed my point.

"You're only interested in being a good patient and pleasing these doctors who won't ever see you again once they finish."

"What?! Are you saying I can't think for myself about what I need? That I can't stand up for myself?"

He denied it but kept challenging me about how I try to appease and please whenever I'm under pressure. He grew more determined.

"I am NOT going to consent to them planting a ticking time bomb in you because you don't want to make waves."

"That is NOT what I'm doing!" The outrage was stealing my breath. I sat straighter. "But I don't think they're trying to scam us into something. If we don't trust our medical team, why have them?"

"I am not just going to blindly accept whatever they say. I don't care how uncomfortable it gets. If it was his wife, I bet he'd find another treatment." Determined to make up for past losses, he refused to accept the impending doom embodied in the consent form.

Stalemate.

Throbbing silence descended our household, pulsing with the pain of isolation from each other. We had never been so deadlocked. Our relationship usually had an ease and safety because we saw the world so similarly. Now we didn't, and that felt perilous. My mind ricocheted with questions about what this impasse meant for our marriage:

What if he discovers he doesn't love me? Am I being disloyal? But what about me—it's my body.

But what if he can't tolerate me standing my ground? What if I'm not strong enough to stand my ground? Am I just going along with the doctors? If I don't stick with their recommendation, am I just going along with him?

And the crumpling thought that seized my whole system: *What if we never again have our closeness?* The doubts and fears were metastasizing through me.

In spite of those doubts, and uncharacteristically, I did not budge from my position that the intensified radiation treatment was the right course of action. Reuel's words that I had a pattern of pleasing and appeasing those in authority had stung, because they were true. It was not like me to take a stand opposite those who were most important to me. Or at least, to not take a direct stand. For most of my life, any exertion of will had to be exercised indirectly, but there was no way to indirectly decide about radiation treatment. I was taking a stand for my health and my freedom, and I was in unfamiliar territory.

Terrified about the price I might have to pay if I exerted my freedom, I was also terrified about the price if I didn't. It looked like a no-win situation. If Reuel's need for an alternative treatment prevailed, then I could lose my health. If my need to follow treatment protocol prevailed, then I could lose my safe-harbor marriage.

How could I risk losing the chance to grow old with this man I had given my closely-guarded heart to? And why was he being such an ass about this, impending doom or not? How were we ever going to repair the rift between us? For the first time, I understood what friends had previously confided to me: that there were times it would be easier not to be married. I was shocked that such a thought had crossed my mind. I didn't want to divorce, but most anything would be easier than the level of tension and strain present when we were in the same room. That had to be the opposite of intimacy.

The stress evidently showed on my face at work when the endocrinologist I worked for asked what was happening. After I explained our stalemate, he gave me his opinion.

"Judy, if my wife had the kind of cancer you did, I would recommend this treatment to her," he said. "But don't take just my word for it." He swept his arm around his book-lined office. "Take a look for yourself in these books and medical journals. Use whichever ones you want."

I took home a stack of three-inch thick medical volumes and spread them across the kitchen table after the kids were in bed. I discovered two things. First, with the kind of cancer

I had, it was likely that it would metastasize and kill me long before leukemia had a chance to develop. Second, I learned I was fascinated by research, a seed of interest that later sprouted in my Ph.D. program. I remained convinced that the additional radiation was the right treatment choice. This time I was not yielding my integrity the way I did with my dad before the wedding. But there was a price to be paid for my firm resolve about the correct treatment for me, and it launched us into one of the most painful periods in our marriage.

Almost twenty-five years after that pivotal point in my development and ultimately our marriage, in a twist of irony, Reuel was the one diagnosed with a blood cancer. When the tumors on his spine were discovered, we had some experience to draw from. We reminded each other how he had that sense way back then, when it was discovered that my thyroid tumor was cancer, that I would be okay. He was right. I had cancer, and I was okay. We were temporarily reassured. Surely the same process would happen again. He had cancer, but he would be okay.

13
Letting Go

In the flush of love's light
we dare be brave
And suddenly we see
that love costs all we are
and will ever be.
Yet, it is only love which sets us free.
—Maya Angelou

Third Week of January

I catch glimpses of Reuel as we head to the hospital again to try yet another type of chemotherapy treatment. The lymphoma is proving to be a formidable foe, defying the chemical weapons we've been hurling at it and ravaging his upper right pelvic bone. These days, Reuel is either restless from pain or listless from pain medication. His world centers around pain, and it's a jealous tyrant, consuming his attention and energy. I'm jealous, too. I don't like that pain preoccupies him, but I don't know how to win him back from this tyrant.

We are desperate for this new chemo cocktail to be the one that knocks out the cancer. After all, we were assured way back at the eagle sighting that it would be okay. (The assurance was similar to what we were given with my cancer diagnosis years before, and look how well that turned out.)

At least here in the hospital I have an ally in the drugs that ease his pain, so he can be more present. We joke with the now-familiar nursing staff and ask about the latest in their families since we were here a few weeks ago. Their faces light up when they see Reuel, and it comforts me to know they like him. Whenever I leave for the office, I feel a little easier knowing they're on his side, pulling for him and giving him extra care.

The charge nurse walks through the door cautiously holding an IV bag covered with orange warning stickers. I remember the guarded way my doctor had carried the liquid radiation canister for my thyroid treatment.

"So, what kind of friendly poisons do you have for me today?" Reuel asks.

She smiles as she hooks the bag to the IV pole. "A fine vintage," she quips, knowing of his wine hobby.

"Good. I don't want to waste this effort on the cheap boxed stuff," he says.

The oncologist enters to give us the latest, poor results of the blood tests. He glances at the biohazard bag, the contents of which are starting to drip into Reuel's veins, and the nurse turns it toward the doctor so he can see the fine print. I'm reminded of a sommelier presenting a bottle of fine wine at the dinner table, label side up, for Reuel's approval. The doc nods his head and asks if we have any questions, but we've been through this drill several times. The only questions I have are ones he can't answer. He says he'll check back later and continues his rounds.

I chat with Reuel and the nurse a bit about the weather and the traffic jams on the highway we can see from his room. A cup of coffee sounds good, so I leave for the family waiting room, where there is always a big thermos of hot coffee. On my way back to the room, I see the oncologist at the station writing up notes. We make eye contact, and he motions me to where he is standing.

"We are beginning to run out of chemical options," he says, looking me in the eye.

"Then what?" I try not to sound as alarmed as I feel.

"You know our goal has been to halt the lymphoma enough so that we could harvest your husband's stem cells and transplant them back into his 'clean' system. We wanted to avoid radiation because that would make doing the stem-cell transplant impossible. Remember that the stem-cell transplant offers the best prognosis for remission. But radiation may be our only hope now."

He is waiting for a response, so I nod my head. I've not forgotten that our goal has been the stem-cell transplant.

"There is maybe one more chemo treatment we can try if this one doesn't work." My mind fuses to the words "one more" as the doctor goes on. "But his pain level concerns me. It appears to come from the area on his hip where we haven't been able to arrest the lymphoma."

"What would radiation do?"

"It could halt the lymphoma in that site, but then he would not qualify for the stem-cell transplant." The doctor pauses, presumably to see if I have more questions. I am frozen in my tracks in the middle of the cancer ward, styrofoam coffee cup in hand. He must be used to the blank stares that follow such serious conversations. "Well," he says, "we'll hope this next one works. But we may have to consider radiation."

"Yes, of course," I'm finally able to utter. Of course? As if that were the most logical step in this falling-through-the-rabbit-hole experience we're in. What else will we have to let go of? My

stomach knots at the thought of proceeding with radiation. Then a
memory is nudged loose. I'm probably feeling what Reuel felt, all
those years ago, about my own radiation.

Inside Look: Case Consultation Between
Client Sessions, Later Career

It wasn't often that my colleague Resmaa's schedule and mine lined up so that we had a free hour between our clients. We had been eager to check in with each other, so he came across the hall into my office and we bemoaned the challenges of working with couples. Not only did we share an office suite, but we also did co-therapy with some client couples, an exciting and energizing venture for us both. At first glance, perhaps to some we wouldn't have appeared to be so compatible— African-American Resmaa, living in the North side of Minneapolis, committed to the health and healing of his community; Scandinavian-looking me, living in a suburb, committed to the healing of couples who showed up in my office. But when we did therapy together, we had an immediate synchronicity of purpose even while pursuing it from different angles.

"Why do you think we work so well together?" I asked.

He didn't hesitate. "Because we've both done our own work on our marriages. It becomes apparent when someone has or hasn't done their work."

"I agree! I've worked with some therapists who hadn't done their own work, and we just spun our wheels with the client couple. That hasn't happened when you and I do co-therapy because we seem to know intuitively where we're going. But I was wondering, after that last session we had with The Grays, how would you put into words what we try to do with couples?"

He thought for a moment, looked up, and exclaimed, "We try to grow them up!" I barely got my coffee swallowed, and then we both burst into laughter. "Isn't that what we had to do in our own marriages, was to grow up and be adults? To let go of acting like kids?"

I got quiet. Resmaa noticed I was no longer laughing. "What's up, Sis?"

"I just remembered one of the first times I was faced with letting go in order to grow up. Ugh!" I smiled at his nod of understanding. "No wonder our client couples resist and struggle. It's hard!"

....

When I was thirty years old and Reuel and I were in our standoff about my thyroid treatment, I drove home from work on a snowy January evening, dreading going into the house. Home with Reuel had always been such a refuge, but in the midst of our dissonance, the space between us had turned cold and silent. Three rambunctious children cushioned the sharp edges of separateness, but once they were in bed, we were left with the pain of isolation.

On that night in the car, my stomach hurt with that dread, so I didn't mind the traffic snarls from Washington

D.C.'s unusual snowfall that would delay my arrival home.
I turned on the radio and heard "breaking news" slashing
across the airwaves. An Air Florida jet had just crashed into
the 14th Street Bridge, a few miles from where I was stuck in
traffic. Eyewitness accounts described smashed cars on the
bridge, bodies being counted, and rescues in the icy river. My
heart dropped as the tragic story developed. Suddenly I felt
an urgency to get home. Nothing was more important, at that
point, than hugging my family.

I finally pulled into the drive, flew out of the car and
up the steps into the house. Reuel, watching for me, flung
open the door to enfold me in his arms. We clung to each other
while the older two preschoolers bobbed by our legs until the
baby cried for his own cuddling. As we untangled, I wondered
briefly if this jolting reminder of the unpredictability of life
would warm the chill between us. I had not changed my mind
about what should be done.

Reuel had dinner ready. We took our places around
the table and joined hands for prayer, including the baby's
wiggling hand from the high chair in our circle. *This is what
matters most to me,* I thought, catching Reuel's eye as one of
the kids thanked God for the mashed potatoes. I could see the
same emotion in his eyes. We believed that relationships are
life, but recently our beliefs about how to extend that life could
not have been further apart. Time was running out. A medical
decision needed to be made.

A few nights later, when I returned home from work,
Reuel once again had dinner made. This time, though, he
stopped and looked at me.

"Can we go into the other room?" he asked. I steeled

myself. "Today when I was praying," he began, "I realized that I had to let go of this. It's your body, and I have to trust you to make the decisions for it."

I looked at him, wondering if there was a "but" en route.

"Whatever you choose," he said, "I will support with no hard feelings. I am still terrified I will lose you, but this has to be your decision."

I began to weep, whether from relief that we had a decision or from the enormity of the gift Reuel had just offered. He had let go, despite his fears. Now we both could honor the strength of my convictions. Tearful, Reuel tentatively held out his arms. I leapt into them, and we hugged as if we'd returned from a long absence.

"I know it's scary," I said softly, tears still streaming, "but I've really researched this. The kind of cancer I have would kill me long before I ever got leukemia from the radiation. I believe the best decision is to eliminate whatever that thyroid material is." There it was. I held my truth in the face of this man I desperately loved and wanted to please. I stood taller.

The decision finally made, medical orders commenced, and I was hospitalized within a week. I was admitted to a private room because I had to be quarantined due to the level of radiation, but I was not prepared for what I encountered when I walked into my room. Every surface I was likely to touch—light switch, telephone, even the toilet—was swathed in plastic wrap. The new nightgown I'd gotten for the occasion was sent home with Reuel. I had to strip off everything I wore and replace it with hospital garb, because everything I touched, dripped, leaked, or sweated on would become radioactive.

"Don't touch anything you don't need to," drilled the technician. I flinched, and he tried to soften his approach. "Don't worry. I'll be in three times a day to read you with a Geiger counter."

In a flash of uncertainty, I questioned my decision, my motivations (was I just being stubborn?), my research capabilities. My eyes darted around the Saran-wrapped room in which I would be trapped for the next three or four days. My heart beat faster, my mind raced: Can people—me, specifically—go crazy in quarantine? I had wanted some time to myself, but really! Was this one of those careless prayers God answered? As the church elders said, "Be careful what you ask for."

The technician must have seen the near-panic on my face, so he explained more. He showed me the hazmat suit he'd wear the next time he came to the room and told me how many decades it would take to break down the radiation in the socks I wore. He saved his best reassurance for last, saying, "I was one of the first on the scene after the Three Mile Island disaster!"

Was I about to become a disaster?

I caught up on my reading during the hospital stay and didn't go stir-crazy, although I was tempted to paint the walls with my radioactive hands just to be oppositional. I savored the time for reflection.

As one part of my body was being irradiated, another part of me was being born. I had ridden on Reuel's coattails the past ten years, and I liked it back there. It fit the gender-role template of the 1950s and early 60s, when I was a girl. But I was beginning to realize it wasn't honest, it wasn't responsible, and it wasn't mature. How easy it was to direct and criticize from the coattails of a strong person shielding me. It was another thing entirely to stand on my own. It was time to emerge from his shadow. I decided to choose not only life, but also full adulthood.

14
What-Ifs

Late January, Early February

Life is perplexing right now. I have many fears, but I also believe the next course of chemo will be effective. The fear and the belief ricochet inside me. I'm learning to live with both. Facing the painful possibilities keeps me out of desperate denial about the gravity of our situation. I can't stand to be one of those women in utter denial. At the same time, my belief in the effectiveness of the next treatment keeps me from collapsing in despair. I can barely tolerate the thought that the medicine might not save my husband.

I have done periodic, personal reality checks since Reuel's prognosis went from bad to worse. They help me feel like I'm in control. Now it's January, and part of me is amused at how ridiculous my illusion of control is. Still, I start my check-in today by taking stock. Yes, this is serious. Stage-IV non-Hodgkin's lymphoma is deadly. Reuel could die. But Reuel is a fighter. He is strong spiritually. He hasn't been given any hint that he'll die, and at the beginning, he was told it would be okay. Am I foolish for having hope? The research suggests that positive thinking and prayers might help a patient. If they can change even the structure of water crystals, sure-

ly they can help Reuel! I wonder if I'm dredging up false belief to coat a truth I don't want to accept. I scan my body to see if it is holding a different reality, like some tension or pain that belies how I'm really feeling. No, things seem consistent. The tension fits with the stress of this situation.

Fear of the worst and hope for the best continue to ping-pong in my mind. I wonder if I'm succumbing to false hope, then wonder what could be false about hope. I believe, but what if I'm delusional to hold fast to the idea that this next application may be the magic bullet? I believe it anyway. His battle is taking longer than we expected, and he'll have more to recover from, but he will recover. This feels like truth, and a sense of peace calms my body and mind. Okay, check-in done for now.

I look over at Reuel, enthroned in The Bahamas by the big windows where, in waking moments, he can look out at the deer and muskrat tracks in the snow. His eyes are closed, and I wonder if he's asleep or overwhelmed, when he lifts one eyelid to look at me with that familiar half-smile.

"How ya doin'?" How many times have I posed that question in our almost thirty-five years of marriage?

His smile spreads across his face, his eyes close, and he waggles his eyebrows. "Life is good in The Bahamas when the narcotics kick in," he says.

Now I wonder how many times through the years he has used his eyebrows as punctuation marks. They could mean anything from "Gotcha!" to sharing a secret in a room full of people to "Meet me in the bedroom." The chemo hasn't fazed the expressiveness of his eyebrows, despite defoliating the rest of his head, now covered with a soft beret to retain some body heat. He must sense me looking at him and opens his eyes.

"What are you thinking?" he asks, that perpetual question that I both loved and dreaded dating back to courting days. Today I'm not sure how honest to be, especially after my own check-in, but he always knows when I'm holding out on him.

"A couple of things. Did you ever think you'd need to wear a hat in the house to stay warm?" He's notorious for running hot even in the winter. He shakes his head, like that's a good one.

"But then I wondered if the reason you've been so warm is that the lymphoma was starting. Remember how all the medical people kept asking if you had night sweats?" I don't want to sound like I'm accusing him of not catching this cancer earlier. But maybe I am.

He pauses to consider, eyes down, then looks up at me. "I don't know," he says with a penetrating look that lets me know he has considered the possibility. "I'm not sure we ever will know. How is that for you?"

"Rather awful. My mind goes to all these what-if places, like what if you hadn't put fertilizer on the lawn? Or what if you were exposed to some carcinogenic material in Barbados? Or what if you hadn't sprayed for spiders under the deck to protect me from another brown recluse bite?" I hear myself sounding a little frantic.

He holds out his hand, and I kneel beside the recliner so we're on eye level.

"I know," he says quietly. "I've asked the Divine about that, but I haven't gotten anything. I think if there was something important for us to know, we would know." We are silent, absorbing the truth of it. After a few moments, I shift gears.

"Well, the other thing I was thinking about was how lucky I am you aren't like the husbands I hear complaints about. No, make that how lucky you are that you're not like those other husbands," I tease, standing up, ready to get him another glass of water.

"Isn't that what I've always told you?" His eyes try to twinkle as the narcotics swing into full effect. Soon he's asleep, his face temporarily free of pain.

I was going to tell him about the friends and clients who complain about their husbands being whiners. Reuel has never been a whiner, never goes into "poor me" mode when he gets a cold or the flu, although he can be pretty obnoxious whenever he wants his back scratched. But when it comes to pain, there haven't been the usual moans and groans, so it has taken me a while to realize how severe his pain has been. What if I had paid more attention? Could we have caught this earlier?

He snorts a sleepy little snort in the chair, and then his forehead creases. It is impossible to miss the waves of pain that cross his face or the constant shifting in The Bahamas to find a more comfortable position. I hope the medication will give him a good three hours of relief, but I realize with a sinking feeling that his limit has been closer to two.

A few days later, his best friend Doug calls. He's planning to come for a visit this weekend. Reuel's face lights up, and I suddenly realize how he's changed: His color is a waxy yellow since the last chemo, his face looks permanently drawn by the intractable pain, and he walks with a cane because his hip can't support the weight of his shrinking body. A visit from Doug—a stained-glass artist who shares a powerful spiritual connection to Reuel—will be good therapy.

When Doug and his wife, Geri, arrive, Reuel's eyes overflow. He manages to stand so he can hug his friend—no small feat since Doug is almost a foot shorter. After sitting around the table with mugs of coffee, catching up, Reuel needs to move back to The Bahamas. As he makes his way there, Doug slips out, returning with a hefty box. He carefully sets it on the table, every eye watching as he reveals the contents. Doug had told me what he was bringing, so I watch Reuel. Doug lifts a stunning stained-glass lampshade from the box, and Reuel's eyes widen as if he can't quite comprehend. Then they fill with tears again.

"W-w-what?" he barely speaks.

"This is for your wine cellar. Tarrah designed it, so it's one-of-a-kind," Doug explains, referring to his artistic daughter. "I picked each piece of glass to hold a special meaning, and you always said that when you had a wine cellar, you wanted a stained-glass lamp-shade in it." Doug points to the burgundy-colored grape clusters that dangle from the edge of the shade. It is exquisite.

When Reuel speaks, he is surprisingly firm. "That's not going down in the wine cellar until I can walk down there and enjoy it. Judy, can you find a table and a lampstand so I can see it here?"

I scramble to find something suitable and bring from the basement a lampstand and his grandmother's antique sewing chest with its multitude of drawers and cubbyholes. We gingerly set the new lamp on it and move the table at an angle so Reuel can enjoy its intricacies from The Bahamas.

After a good weekend that left us all tired from the intense emotions, it's time for Doug and his wife to leave. I walk them to the back door. We embrace in an unexpectedly tearless hug—we may have drained our reservoirs of tears—and Doug shakes his head. "Reuel looks so different . . ." he starts, then trails off and walks to his car.

A week has passed now, and another friend, a trauma specialist, is visiting. Sharon is gifted at healing the effects of trauma in the body and spirit and seems to know just how to use questions and visual imagery. She had volunteered to see if she could help reduce Reuel's pain by processing any trauma through visual imagery. Reuel is willing. He knows from previous experience the relief provided by this approach.

Sharon stands at his feet, which are propped up in the recliner, and looks at him carefully, taking in his changes since she saw him last. They hold each other's gaze in silence for several moments. *I wonder if the healing is already starting. What kinds of energies are being exchanged? The air feels charged.* Reuel's eyes are getting misty. He and Sharon continue to communicate in silence, her hands holding his sock-covered toes.

Finally she speaks and asks him to visualize the pain in his body.

"It's everywhere, moving all over."

"Okay," she says, "but I want you to actually visualize its shape as it moves around in you, and the color, and anything else you see."

He is silent for a while, eyes closed, face tilted up as he scans the interior of his body. I watch him, glancing occasionally at Sharon for direction, because I'm not sure if he's fallen asleep. She seems content to let the silence continue, so I wait also.

Then Reuel speaks. "It's round," he says and continues haltingly. "Round . . . big, about six inches . . . yellowish and pretty thick, about five-and-a-half inches in diameter." He pauses. Sharon and I look at each other and grimace at the visual he's providing. "The pain makes me want to tell the docs to irradiate NOW. Kill the tumor NOW. I'm afraid the docs will just tell me, 'Either way, you're dead.'"

We are silent. Sharon and I alternately glance at each other *and Reuel. Then he speaks again.*

"All the pain reminds me of being dead . . . I want to trust the Divine in this, but when the physical pain overwhelms everything else, I wonder if it overwhelms the Divine, also." Tears slide down his cheeks.

"Ok," Sharon responds with energy, "what is it you'd like to do to that thick, yellow tumor?"

Reuel opens his eyes and looks at her, confused. "What do you mean?"

"I want you to visualize that pain, that tumor, and then visualize how you'd like to change the look of it, or the size, or anything else you'd like to see. And while you do that, I want you to use the tac scan," she instructs, referring to the bilateral-stimulation machine used by trauma specialists to help kindle emotional and physical processing.

He puts on the headphones and adjusts the speed and volume of the beeps that alternately sound in each ear. Then he closes his eyes and gets very still in the recliner. Every few minutes he opens an eye to adjust the tac scan, then quickly goes back into a trance-like state.

Suddenly his eyes fly open, he sits up, and gasps, "Wow!"

Sharon and I eagerly wait to hear what happened, but it takes Reuel a few minutes to gather himself to speak. He seems to be sorting through things in his head. Sharon asks if the pain has changed.

"Oh yeah," he says, like it's an understatement. "I got a firm picture of the pain, and as the tac scan beeped, the shape of the pain began to change. It started shrinking until it became the size of a quarter."

Relief courses through me. Maybe this is part of the healing we've been expecting!

"Were there any other changes?" Sharon asks.

"The pain changed color. It began shifting, the yellow fading out and then turning into the most beautiful shade of blue. In fact, it's the same blue as the sea in Barbados."

Yes! I know that an association to Barbados carries tremendous healing properties for Reuel. I glance at Sharon, but she doesn't seem surprised.

"How is the pain now?" she asks.

"It's much less. There's hardly any pain, compared to what it was."

"Then let's lock that in," she says, and directs him to visualize his favorite things from the island. He falls asleep to images of the beach, the sun, the sand, and the ocean. I can see him drinking it all in, warming him clear to his marrow. I am warmed also, and for the time being, my what-ifs recede.

15
Hearts

"We take turns at being the offender and the offended until our very last breath. It's reassuring to know that we have the possibility to set things right, or at least to know that we have brought our best selves to the task at hand, however the other person responds."
—Harriet Lerner

Mid-February

It is a few days after Reuel's visualization of the pain shrinking, and we've come to Valentine's Day, typically cold and blustery. Reuel is pretty much bound to The Bahamas, even sleeping there at night now since he can't manage stairs. The healing and elimination of pain from the visualization process appears to have been temporary, and I am secretly crushed. With that technique, I really thought we had our miracle. I realize in some part of my consciousness that this isn't the first time I've expected a miracle since he was diagnosed. It is also not the first time I have been disappointed, but I don't want to consider right now what that might mean. After all, it's Valentine's Day.

I stop by a restaurant after work to pick up our Valentine's Dinner, thinking about the contrast between the carry-out bags in my hand and previous Valentine evenings spent in French restaurants with Reuel's carefully chosen wine. I sigh and then remember to be grateful that at least we can be together. I wonder how he has been managing the pain this afternoon.

Not so well, it appears. The pain is gaining ground so that even his appetite is affected, unusual for Reuel. He declines the wine he just asked me to fetch from the cellar, remembering the narcotics already in his system. I give him a card and hold him as best I can while leaning over the recliner. He apologizes for not having a card for me.

"What, no card? What have you been doing?" I'm rewarded with a brief smile.

We watch a little American Idol. I clean up the kitchen and am rapidly feeling ready for bed. I tease him about wishing he were coming upstairs with me, but instead of his usual playful response, he asks me to help line up his meds for the night. I try to decipher his log of the times he takes each prescription but have trouble reading his shaky handwriting. We strategize together until we have each pill designated at the appropriate times to get him through the night, lining them up like infantry on the side table next to a tall glass of water. I make sure his cell phone is beside him so he can call me if needed. His voice is now so weak he stands no chance of waking me in my notoriously heavy sleep.

Somewhere around 2:30 a.m. the phone rings, and Reuel says, "Please come." I run downstairs to find him writhing on the recliner.

"I can't do it any longer," he gasps. "I've got to go to the hospital."

My heart is pounding heavily. I check the medication log to see if he needs another pain pill, and my heart drops into my stomach. He has already taken all the pills we laid out, meant to last him for several more hours.

"Can you wait until I shower?" I ask, hesitant to even pose

*the question. The reality is that if I'll be going into the office from the
emergency room, I better get showered and dressed accordingly. He is
in tremendous pain, despite who knows how much excess medication
is in him, and here I am thinking about my "normal" life at the office
and the clients scheduled for the day.*

"Yeah, I think I can wait, if you can help me get to the bathroom."

*I lower the footrest on the recliner, but the pain is too great for
him to tolerate the shift in position.* Dear God, I silently plead, how
on earth will we get him to the van? *I run to get him a container
so he can relieve his bladder without any more immediate pain.*

*I race through my shower, throw on makeup and clothes, and
come back down the steps to find him leaning heavily on his cane, but
standing. How did he do that? I wonder about it, offer a "Thank you,
God," and focus on positioning myself under his arm to support his
weak side. After we take the first step together, he abruptly reaches
into his pocket, grabs something in his hand, and puts it in the drawer of the nearby stand. Before I can ask about it, he gasps as a new
wave of pain overtakes him. Feelings of helplessness flood me as we
warily, ploddingly make our way.*

*Somehow, we get into the van and are now driving to the hos-
pital. I have no awareness of how we stumbled through the long, dark
hall, into the tiny laundry room with its awkward angles, down two
steps into the icy garage and minivan whose engine is unenthusiastic
to turn over in the Minnesota winter. I shoot another thanks heav-
enward even as I pull up to the ER doors and frantically run inside,
leaving Reuel in the car with the motor running.*

"I need help to get my husband inside," *I cry to the first person I find. I turn to race back to the van, expecting they'd be right on
my heels. But my emergency is not theirs, so they look for help and a*

wheelchair at a more leisurely pace than my heart is beating.

Once we're in the intake room, I wonder why they can't just take the information in the records from the last time we made this trip, not many weeks ago. I grab the gallon Ziploc bag of medication I have learned to bring with us to every hospital visit, and the ER nurse makes her way through the bounty of brown pill bottles, entering the data from the labels into the electronic records.

Reuel is almost jumping out of his skin with pain, and his responses to the nurse's questions take on a tone of desperation. He is desperate because he is so dependent on medication to tolerate consciousness, which means he is dependent on medical personnel to believe him. I watch him with a creeping feeling of dread as he begins to give them any remotely relevant data about his condition, frantically hoping to convince them of his need.

When the intake nurse steps out of the room, I murmur to him, "It's okay. They don't need that much information." He wells up with tears, muffles a sob, and says, "I'm so afraid they won't believe me."

The triage nurse returns and wheels him to one of the ER rooms, where they begin to manage his pain. After a number of injections takes the edge off, Reuel's body begins to relax. His face softens. Soon he's dozing. I finally breathe deeply, even if the breath is filled with alcohol and antiseptic aromas. I'm tired, and I'm also aware I haven't fully let in what I'm feeling emotionally. It's not necessary to completely realize that right now, I reason, and am okay with that. After all, I am not the one combating cancer and enduring onslaughts of pain. I'd much rather be the one, I reflect with a morsel of guilt, to make sure the management of our lives continues by paying bills, shuttling to medical appointments, updating friends through the Caring Bridge site, and continuing to see clients both for their sakes and my own.

The ER doc returns and Reuel rouses slightly. "We're going to admit you back to the oncology unit so we can get this pain under control," he explains. Nurses enter and start arranging tubes and bags of his belongings for transport. I move out of their way, then notice Reuel looking at me. I take his hand. He squeezes it just hard enough to communicate. Then we ride the elevator into the trenches.

Inside Look: Marriage and Family Therapy (MFT) Classroom, Later Career

"Class, I know our topic today is couple conflict, but before we get into the many ways conflict appears, and what to do when it does, I wanted to share what happened yesterday in a client session. When you were little and you had a spat with your sibling or a neighbor kid, what did your parents tell you to do to make it right?" They almost unanimously said they were told to say they were sorry.

"Exactly, and did that help? Maybe sometimes? Maybe sometimes not so much?

"The client situation I referred to involved an apology, or at least that's what it was supposed to be. The husband had had an affair, and he suddenly decided to apologize to his wife. I didn't know he was going to do that, or I would have coached him first. Unfortunately, he ticked all the boxes of what an apology is not. Here are some of the things he said:

'I'm sorry, but if you hadn't been so cold . . .'
'What am I supposed to do, apologize for being hu-

man? For not being perfect?'

'I'm sorry. Can we just drop it now and move on?'

'Geez, can you just quit crying? When are you going to get over it? I said I'm sorry.'

"So how do you think his apology worked out? If you think it may have made things worse, you're right.

"What was wrong with his apology? Call them out, and I'll list them."

Students share as I write on the board: Blaming his wife. Too general, not specific. His timetable, not hers. No empathy for what she's feeling. Thought he could use a formula to fix it.

"Yes, good points. And this is what I would have coached him against, had I known. He was not ready to apologize, he just wanted to get past this pain. Unfortunately, it served to break her heart even more. He's confused since he thought he was supposed to apologize and seek forgiveness, and now they're further apart than ever."

....

The thing about intimacy is that we have to lay our hearts bare in order to be known. And that means our hearts will get wounded. Or our scar tissue from previous wounds will be revealed. It's inevitable that we will both wound and be wounded. Usually, we won't intend to hurt our partners, but it happens. The good news is that marriage—really any committed relationship—has the potential to heal wounds rooted in childhood. Unfortunately, it also can inflict our deepest wounds. When that happens, how does one begin to heal?

First, by finding any scrap of courage within, or to act "as if" you found courage even when you didn't (sort of a "fake-it-til-you-make-it" approach). Courage is required in order to do something different: breathing instead of reacting, being vulnerable instead of bluffing, or maybe listening compassionately. It takes guts to face the pain of old wounds or even fresh ones, but it is necessary and so worth it. The pain of confronting yourself—and maybe your partner—is a pain that can lead to healing and health. It's a lot like a sliver in a child's finger. She doesn't want her mother to dig it out because it hurts. But if she ignores it, her finger swells, throbs, gets infected, and ends up hurting even more. Avoiding pain—whether physical or emotional—may only increase it.

Reuel had told me on many occasions how much better his life was after we married. But he didn't confront me about the ways he was still in emotional pain until almost three decades into it. One day, he finally told me that for much of our marriage, he didn't feel chosen and prioritized by me. Some of that was on his side of the fence, never fully letting in my love, like what he realized with my happiness for him over the granite countertops. Some of it was on my side of the fence. The way I took on tasks, went back to school, studied, volunteered at church or in professional groups, and maxed out my schedule with clients . . . all of these commitments left very little time and energy for him. Reuel always asked how he could help me, and I always had suggestions. What he wasn't able to say at the time was how neglected he felt.

By the time he confronted me, his old wounds caused by neglect triggered my old wounds (perfection and needing to please). When he brought it up, I bristled and rejected his complaint as childish.

"Why didn't you tell me then? What am I supposed to do now?"

"I wish I had told you," he said. "It was my failure to trust you, to trust that you would listen and respond. I'm sorry."

That lowered my defenses. "I'm sorry you felt neglected." His head pulled back. "No, wait."

His reaction helped me realize the level of blame loaded into my apology. How could I accept rather than avoid my responsibility? "I'm sorry I overscheduled myself. I'm sorry for the times when I gave you reason to not trust I'd listen and respond." I checked inside to see what else I needed to own up to with honesty. Reuel watched me.

I continued. "I can see how my over-scheduling and assumption of your help could leave you feeling taken for granted, how you took a back seat to my busy-ness." He nodded. "I can also see how that paralleled your parents' lack of attention and neglect and how you suffered for it."

"Yes," he responded, "and in childhood, I couldn't say anything about it, or I would have been punished and neglected even more." He paused for a moment. "And I'm sorry I treated you as if you were my parent. I know you aren't, and I know you aren't a punishing person."

"Thank you." My heart opened to him. "I'm sorry for behaving anywhere near that dynamic from your childhood."

We hugged then, because we needed to catch our breaths from the emotional heavy lifting. I realized later that he hadn't said anything in response to my apologies. I let it go, wondering if this would be like the granite, taking a while for him to accept or let in my regret.

One Sunday morning over coffee, Reuel said he'd been thinking more about our exchange. I could see by his pinched eyes and mouth that this was difficult for him. I refilled my coffee mug and took a seat across the round table from him. He stared out at the pond and I waited. I knew by now that we would make our way through whatever it was he needed to say.

He began. "I learned not to trust forgiveness because it changed nothing and soon everything was back to normal. Spiritually, forgiveness was never permanent, so you could be forgiven one day and be on the road to hell the next day. I now understand and believe forgiveness can be permanent, but it wasn't then, not to me."

"What happened back then, that you learned to not trust forgiveness?"

"Two of the most damaging experiences were, first, all the times I was forced to ask for my mother's forgiveness when I believed I hadn't done anything wrong. That was then compounded by the second thing: I couldn't tell my parents that they needed to ask for my forgiveness when they mistreated and abused me.

"Then, when I was meditating this morning, I understood that I never felt forgiven by my dad for being who I was. Due to his abuse and my never measuring up in his eyes, I constantly lived with the belief that I needed to be forgiven for something, and his forgiveness never came. As painful as that was, the insight was also quite liberating."

"I think I get that. It's like it's not really about you, but about your dad."

"Yes, exactly! It's a relief." His smile was more relaxed, but not back to normal.

"Is there more?"

"Yeah, this next part is harder to explain. On a gut level, I haven't trusted your words when you asked for forgiveness, because I didn't believe things would really change, and I thought I'd feel pain again over and over."

I inhaled, ready to speak, but he cut me off.

"I know, I know—no relationship is without pain or repeated patterns. But when you would do something all over again, I found reason to have my belief system confirmed. I could believe you meant well at the time, but I believed the patterns would continue."

I shifted in my chair, hoping I could keep my defensiveness at bay. He seemed to see my tension and continued.

"So once again, as in my first family, I believed more in the patterns of pain than in change and forgiveness. The pain was more reliable than forgiveness. Even as I tell you this, it seems pretty messed up, but that's what I grew up with. I believe differently now about forgiveness, so now I get to translate that into our relationship."

I wasn't sure where to go from there. I reached across the table for his hand. "What do you believe differently now?"

"Oh, my. Well, I can tell you what divine forgiveness feels like. Freedom from fear. Release. Joy. Fulfillment. It feels empowering."

"Yes, and that's how I experience our marriage," I softly replied, pained to realize Reuel hadn't experienced it similarly.

I admired him for confronting himself about his pain with regard to forgiveness. I wanted to admire him for confronting me with his truth of feeling neglected in the marriage, but at the time it felt like a sliver had just been dug from my heart.

Who IS This? 16

"Before we marry, we don't recognize that some of the same things that attract us to our partners will eventually have an under-side that tortures us. . . . If we saw it coming, no one would ever get married and the human race would die out."
—James W. Maddock

Mid-to-Late February

On February 15th, the day after Reuel was admitted, I stop by the hospital before my office hours. I enter his room with a latte in hand, only to discover two nurses, an aide, and Reuel in heated conversation. They are gathered around his bed, where he's propped at a forty-five-degree angle, his voice tight, hands punctuating his words with short, chopping motions, the lines between his eyes deeply creased. The nurses are using soothing voices to explain or appease, but Reuel is having none of it. They glance up at me and look relieved, as if I'll help make sense of this communication breach, but I don't know what is happening. I turn to Reuel first and give him a kiss. His face breaks into a brief smile, then he updates me.

Evidently his pain had spiked in the middle of the night. He had requested more medication—he knew how to manage this by now—but his nurse didn't have orders from the doctor to cover the extra dosage. Reuel was desperate with pain. When the head nurse came on the floor, she tried to resolve the problem. Reuel now turns to the head nurse.

"I understand the nurse couldn't give me any more medication without orders from the doctor," he states slowly but firmly, "but I don't understand why she didn't contact the doctor for further orders."

The head nurse explains the protocol. I nod my understanding and glance at Reuel to see if he gets it. But his face is tightly set, sparks of irritation in his eyes. He is not letting them off the hook.

"There was a breakdown in the overnight communication and follow-through," he speaks very deliberately to the center of the room, then pauses for emphasis. "And I suffered more because of it."

He looks at me then, and I realize how loaded that statement is. He was always the one to suffer the greatest whenever communication broke down or follow-through failed in his family.

Most of the nurses apologize and express their regrets, then leave us to respond to other patients. I ask how he's feeling.

"I'm okay. It just shouldn't have to be this difficult to get what I need, especially after the oncologist ordered as much pain relief as I require." He leans into his pillow farther and breathes more deeply, looking as though he's letting go some of the previous discord.

We chat a while, and then I leave to go to the office.

When I return to visit him later that day, the nurses take me aside to ask about things he told them during the day about his connections to the mafia and a contract out on his life. My mouth falls open. "That was our reaction, too," the nurse responds in relief. "Maybe the narcotics are creating his confusion."

That turns out to be an understatement. From then on, Reuel is not the only one confused. He recognizes Marci and me, enjoys our time together, and even carries on credible conversations about Marci's work and friends. But every once in a while, he drops something into the dialogue that stops us cold, like asking us if we've seen the man in the hospital who's out to get him. Marci and I each catch our breath, widen our eyes in incredulity, and look at each other for our own reality checks. His need for extreme doses of narcotics is impacting his reality as well as his pain.

Every morning, I walk into his room wondering if the fog has cleared. Often, it takes some time before I'm able to determine his lucidity, because he can be so clear one moment and then suddenly lurch into an alternate reality. As time goes on without his return to clarity, I get concerned that the drugs have done permanent damage. The doctors don't have clear answers for me, and I wonder with suppressed panic how confused our medical professionals are.

It has now been two weeks into this medication-induced bizarre world. At least Reuel has stayed sweet, I think to myself, remembering the story of a spouse with a brain tumor who had a drastic personality change complete with belligerence and violence. It could always be worse, I remind myself as I call his room to check on him before I leave the house.

"How are you?" I ask.

"Pretty good," he responds brightly, sounding like his old self. My hopes lift. Maybe he's finally coming out of the drug haze.

"Yeah," he continues, "they're getting ready to move me from radiology to Thursday."

Huh? I try to compute what he just said. From radiology to Thursday? My hopes deflate. I wonder about the strength of the balloon of hope inside me to withstand the daily inflation and leaking. Reuel is waiting for a response, and I muster something standard.

"Well, I hope it's a good trip, and I'll be there in a little while.

Anything you need or would like?"

"No, I'm good," he responds. So, I think as I straighten my shoulders, we're not back to normal yet.

When I enter his room, Reuel is intent on unwinding the coiled phone cord beside his bed.

"Did you bring the adapters?"

"What adapters?"

"The adapters," he emphasizes, like that would explain it. "You know, for the ice cream. So it can come directly into my room."

I can't suppress my smile. Characteristically, he works to find the most efficient method of doing anything!

Marci and I begin to record some of the "Reuel-isms" in a journal we keep in his room, along with our notes to each other about what medical proceedings occur during each one's watch. The humorous ones warm our spirits, but there are serious and poignant moments full of truth and love despite his drug-addled brain.

On Tuesdays we follow American Idol *on television, having as much of a party as we can. We bring popcorn, pull up chairs, invite the nursing staff in, and generally try to create festivity amid the hanging biohazardous bags snaking their toxin-laden tubes toward Reuel's veins.*

His appetite is down, which alarms the staff, but Marci and I discover he enjoys Jamba Juice, so we get him big smoothies whenever we can. Reuel looks forward to the frosty cup. On this day, I have loaded the blend with as much extra nutrition as can be swirled in and wear my gloves to carry the cold smoothie inside from the roaring lion winds which are accompanying March.

As I set it on the tray table, his face lights up, and I know it's not just for the drink. He's glad to see me.

"Pass the used juice?" he asks. Used juice? *Then he abruptly*

folds his hands. I ask what happened.

"We have to wait for the procedure," he explains. "The Jamba Juice procedure." Poor guy, his whole waking world is about procedures.

"The only procedure is to drink it," I state.

"Well okay, then. There you go." It's so typically Reuel.

 ### Inside Look: Counseling Office, Early Career

"She would never have tried to keep me from being with my friends when we were dating! Now I can't even tell my best friend I'll meet him for a beer unless I check with her first. It's like I have to ask permission! What happened to her?"

"What happened to ME? I can't believe you're putting this on me! You're the one who told me that your friends would always come second to what I needed. That lasted a minute, and now you can't wait to get away from me! Was it all a lie?"

Hoo boy. Mr. and Mrs. Smith are at it again, and I am trying desperately to interrupt their same old argument about how the other has changed from their idealized courting days and how that change is somehow a betrayal. Nothing I've tried in previous sessions has made much of a difference, or they wouldn't be in these same fighting positions. Just then I remember something that one of my mentors used to say. I'm not hopeful it will work, but I don't have much to lose at this point.

"You know, it sounds like you each are really

upset that your spouse might have changed from what you knew back when you were dating." They nod. Good.

"Maybe what you didn't realize is that every couple goes through a period when they think they've been 'had.' Every partner at some point believes they've been the victim of a bait-and-switch maneuver. They wonder if they were lied to, and they start to question what was true. Who IS this person I agreed to marry?" They sit up straight in their chairs, eyes wide.

"Remember when you were first falling in love? Everything about your partner was just so perfect, you were both so compatible, and those neuro-hormones were firing off just the right amount of feel-good chemicals. You couldn't imagine then that you'd one day be sitting in my office questioning your judgment." They smile slightly and risk a glance at each other.

"I had a professor who explained it this way. Early in relationships, we all need to have some kind of bait-and-switch bargain operating, even though we aren't even conscious of it, because we need to believe our partner's best advertisement. If we each knew everything there was to know at the outset about our potential partner, we'd all be scared off, and nobody would ever marry!"

By the time I had been married for twenty-eight years, I thought I probably knew everything I needed to know about my husband. I was wrong.

Learning just how much I was mistaken began with an occasion which seemed so innocent (to me), but carried such painful meaning to Reuel that he reactively shoved it underground. There it stayed, gaining energy and absorbing the toxic doubts which thrive in unaware places. By the time this painful piece surfaced and he confronted me a year later, I was stunned. Who WAS this man?

It all started when Reuel's fiftieth birthday was approaching. I wanted to mark the occasion somehow, but we had just signed our lives away to build a new house, so my options were limited. I vetoed a surprise party. He was suffering headaches and body pain that eluded diagnosis. He said his therapy was helping, but I couldn't see that his pain level had been at all dented. I thought a low-key day was in order but needed to check with him.

"Hey, I was thinking about your birthday, the big 5-0. What do you think you'd like to do?"

"Can you believe I'm going to be fifty? Sounds so old. I'm not sure what I want to do. Nothing big. Let me think about it a bit."

The next day, as we were getting ready for bed, he returned to the subject. "I've been thinking about what I want to do for my birthday," he started.

"Good! I'm glad you're putting energy into it, to figure out what you want."

"Well, you know I get the day off, since it's my birthday." He hesitated. "What I'd really like to do is make love five times that day."

"Ha!" burst out of me. Was he serious? He looked serious. *He's got to be kidding!* Was I supposed to wait in bed all day and be at his beck and call? *He can't be serious!*

"Well, you can always dream . . ." I replied as I left to wash my face.

He came into the bathroom to brush his teeth with that tight, angry expression on his face.

I avoided his eyes while I tried to keep my thoughts from spilling out of my mouth. Oh good grief! Now I've done something wrong. Again. Evidently, I was supposed to be excited about his birthday idea. Didn't I get to have my own reactions? Well, I was mad, too. Mad at his presumption, mad that he was mad, mad that he was acting like it was my fault.

Short, choppy movements staccatoed us both into bed. The next morning presented us with more decisions about the new house, and soon the unpleasantness of the previous night was blown away.

A few days later, Reuel's birthday arrived, and I put so much thought into preparing a time to make love that night that I got nervous. *Do I look decent in this new nightgown? Will he find me sexy?* I put some soul music on and placed the two new candles just so. I noticed Reuel had been subdued during the day and wondered what was going through his mind. Whatever it was, this should help. My hands shook as I lit the candles.

Reuel came up from the basement then, took in the efforts I made, and smiled. He reached for me, we embraced, danced a few steps, then began getting down to business. It was an intense time: passionate, sweet, breathless, and loving. We fell into a contented sleep.

The next morning, I was both thankful and relieved that he enjoyed our time. He looked loved, but was he holding something back? I could no longer tell because he seemed pre-occupied more times than not. Was it the house construction, his therapy, the kids becoming adults? His mood generally had turned tense, I realized, and I didn't know if I should do any-thing.

⊠

A year later, I learned what he was holding back. We were in couples therapy again, after a nine-year break. Reuel, over the previous year, had been learning to use his voice, to speak up for himself in ways he never had before. It was a mixed blessing for me. I knew I was supposed to be happy for his positive growth, but it scared me. All at once, what I thought I knew was not necessarily true. His opinions on things from politics to friendships could suddenly switch, and I was powerless to predict which way they would go.

Especially in therapy, I felt helpless about what to expect. How did I brace myself for the upcoming hour's coun-seling session? My shoulders were so tight that bricks could bounce off them. The therapist instructed Reuel to begin. My gut clenched.

"I need to say my truth about something," he said as he turned to me, "because it had a negative effect on me. A year ago, when I turned fifty, I asked to spend the day with you, in bed, making love five times throughout the day."

"Ha!" blurted our therapist.

Oh my God! Our therapist reacted the way I did a year ago. She laughed!

Reuel flinched. His whole body was in recoil.

"Reuel," she appealed, "I might want five dozen roses on my birthday, but that doesn't mean it's realistic. It sounds like a fantasy."

Yes! I felt vindicated after all this time! She also reacted like it was a crazy idea. Then I looked at Reuel, whose face was red, chin high and nostrils flared. Damn, what was going on with him? Uh-oh, he jerked his head toward me.

"Judy, do you feel the same way she does?"

"Well . . . yeah."

Reuel stood and excused himself. He left the room!

Now what? I had been on the therapist end of this sort of situation, but I didn't expect to be the spouse on the receiving end.

The therapist smiled reassuringly at me. "Do you think he just needs some time? Will he be back, or should we end our session?"

How the hell would I know?

Reuel came back then, and said he needed to be going. I had just set another appointment, but he wanted to think about whether he would attend.

Quiet ride home. Quiet dinner. Lots of quiet that night.

I wondered if I should apologize but didn't know what I was sorry for. I was sorry he was so upset, but as much for me as him, so that didn't seem very genuine. And why was he so upset? Did he expect me to think the same way, want the same things he did? I thought we'd already made peace about being different. Whatever it was that impacted him, he looked as if he'd gone to a walled-off place.

I hated that silent, subversive tension. It felt like when we were at an impasse over my thyroid treatment, caught in an underground current of frozen, bitter silence. I didn't know how to reach Reuel, how to thaw him, but it hurt my insides to have this cold block between us.

A few days passed. Or was it a few hours? Time was disrupted when our relationship was. Some of the ice had melted a bit. Reuel finally gathered his inner wherewithal to explain what happened.

"You asked me in our last therapy session to share with the therapist my own healing journey. I started sharing, and then you totally set me up."

"What?" Boom! Totally unexpected gut punch. No way did I set him up.

"That's right. All of a sudden, I wasn't saying the right thing or using the right words. I couldn't tell my own experience without being interrupted by the therapist or by you."

"Uh . . ." Brain fog. I didn't recall interrupting or correcting him in that session.

"I got the message from the both of you that I wasn't doing it right."

Shit! I was not grasping and didn't want to panic. "I'm not understanding . . ."

"I gave an example of something that felt painful to me, but you and the therapist laughed!" His look pierced me. "I ended up shutting down in the session. It felt like anything I said would be used against me."

"Is that why you walked out and why you've felt so far away since then?" I asked. He nodded and turned away. I coached myself to be careful, especially since my heart rate was jumping. I wanted to tell him how wrong he was about that session, but he looked raw and wounded. My heart ached for him, despite how blindsided I felt. I took his hand. "Babe, I am so sorry for how painful that was for you. I didn't realize how awful you felt, or how you felt attacked."

He looked at me, nodded his head once, and squeezed my hand.

A few days later, the overall mood only slightly warmer, he asked if we could pick back up on that conversation. I felt dread.

Reuel stood in the kitchen, head slightly bowed. "A few days ago, when we talked, I didn't let in your empathy and apology when you said it. Instead, what I thought was, 'You should have helped protect me when I was feeling attacked by the therapist . . .' When you understood what I was saying the other night, and apologized, I shut it out. I would not accept it, and wanted to stay cold and angry with you."

Well, he succeeded in that, I thought. Miraculously, a mature part of me prevailed. I asked, "Did something change?"

"Yeah, I finally realized something from childhood—how much I had to shut off my feelings in hopes that my parents would love me. I had to be *not* me in order to be loved, but then I was never loved for who I was." He took a big breath before he continued. "I was terrified of being lost—to myself and to anyone who might love me. But here's the thing," he persisted. "What happened in that therapy session a few days ago was like my worst nightmare. The thought of not being accepted or loved by you was so terrifying that I shut down so I didn't have to feel it."

We sat in silence for a few moments. Who WAS this man who kept revealing more of himself and his heartbreaking childhood? I glanced at my clammy hands, tried to swallow, knew I had to say something, but feared to risk his unacceptance once again.

"How very awful for you! It sounds agonizing." *Please believe me*, I thought-prayed. *Please know this comes from the bottom of my heart.* "I am so, so sorry."

He reached for my hand. "What I have to do," he took a slow, deep breath, "is be known. I have to be known to you and by you." Another pause while he looked first at me, then down, then back into my eyes. "I have to know, to trust, that you will really love ME."

I jumped up to hug him. "I love YOU! I may not be very good at it sometimes, but I love YOU." I paused with the sudden realization that this moment demanded total honesty if he was going to trust me. "Even if I don't *like* something you do, I *love* you."

He softly wept. After a moment he said, "It's all I ever really wanted."

Relief

"Every inch of Mother Earth holds a specially energized connection
to some living creature, and is therefore to be honored."
—Jamie Sams & David Carson

Early March

*We wait for the oncologist to make his morning rounds, and soon
he greets us in his freshly pressed shirt and coordinated tie. Almost
three weeks into this hospitalization, I notice that he looks at me now,
instead of Reuel, to explain the latest blood-level counts and state-of-
the-patient report. Gradually, I have become the authority to consult
for medical procedures. The doctors and nurses continue to speak to
Reuel, but when an okay is needed, their heads turn to me. They wait
for my nod of permission, not Reuel's. He is not fully capable of informed consent, I realize, and swallow the bubble of unease that slips
from my stomach as I focus on what the oncologist is saying.*

*"The lymphoma on your husband's upper pelvic bone is vora-
ciously eating through bone and marrow. I think it is time to consider
radiation."*

*I catch my breath. "But . . ." I'm not sure if I thought it or
said it aloud. The doctor knows my objection and speaks to it before I*

say anything else.

"Yes, it destroys the chance for stem-cell transplantation but so does the advancing lymphoma. Also, we are not able to manage his pain. You see all the different medications we have tried and their effects. Bone cancer is extremely painful. I think radiation is our next best option. It will stop or slow the lymphoma and provide some pain relief."

My face freezes at the starkness of this report. My eyes find Reuel's. He studies first me, then the doctor. After a moment, he nods his head, then looks at me for the final decision. He knows I am more capable than he is at this point. And he trusts me unreservedly.

The burden of the choice threatens to overwhelm me. I can't make this deal-breaker decision by myself! Throughout our thirty-five years together, Reuel and I talked over every major decision, but now he's unable to. I glance between him and the physician as each awaits my response. How can I—so good at avoiding decisions of sole responsibility—be the one in charge? A noise from the hospital corridor brings me back to the present. I must face up to the decision. What options are there, really?

"Of course," I sigh. "Let's start the radiation and get him some relief."

Relief doesn't come at once, of course. Our first trip to radiation teaches us that each radiation treatment requires moving Reuel from bed to gurney to treatment table, causing unbearable suffering for him and agony for me as I watch helplessly.

Today we must avoid repeating that anguish of transfer. The oncology staff aren't equipped to deal with a 6'4", 195-lb man whose size-thirteen feet hang over the end of the bed, so we have to wait for three more able bodies to move Reuel to the gurney. In anticipation of this, Reuel and I had strategized how to get just the right amount of painkiller into him at just the right time to ease the pain of the transfer. By the time the transport team arrives, we have accomplished our goal: Reuel is wearing that slightly sloppy smile that comes with even the briefest relief from pain. Now he closes his eyes, and I hold my breath as the aides grab his underlying blanket.

"One, two, three, MOVE."

Reuel's body slides to a smooth stop on the gurney: no jerks, no winces. He opens his eyes, smiles, and gives everyone a thumbs-up signal. The whole room exhales. The aides smile and joke with him now as they hang the IV-bag and tuck his medical chart in the wire basket at the head of the bed.

I gather my things and move aside for them to wheel the gurney around the sharp angle of the door and into the hall. As the head of the bed swings toward me to get into position, Reuel grabs my hand. We hold hands in our locked and familiar position while staff bustle around us. Just as the bed driver says, "Okay, Mr. Tiesel, let's go," Reuel presses his three middle fingers, one at a time, into my hand. Then he gently releases it as he's wheeled out to the elevator.

I turn away and burst into tears. From deep within, Reuel had drawn on the secret code we had had since before we were engaged: three fingers, pressed one at a time into whatever part of us is available . . . a shoulder during a movie or a back rub, an arm when jostling our way through a crowd, even my swollen belly when Reuel telegraphed to me and the baby inside. Each finger communicates a word: "I" – "love" – "you."

I am undone by his love. His hospital room clears, and I am left blessedly alone. I grab the box of tissues by Reuel's bed, collapse into the hard vinyl chair, and weep. How can I feel so adored and so afraid at the same time?

Despite all the places Reuel's mind wanders during these

dizzying, drugged days, our relationship remains intact. Our deep roots of devotion are anchoring his core and protecting his spirit. His lucidity may meander, but his heart and intention are securely fixed to me, the Divine, and our three children. This love sustains him despite the effects of unspeakable pain and unpredictable medication. It does the same, in turn, for me.

Inside Look: MFT Classroom, Mid-Career

We are midway through the week of an intensive module on "Ethics in Marriage & Family Therapy," and my job is to condense a semester of ethical training into five full days. At least we are in a newer classroom with floor-to-ceiling windows where the A/C keeps pace with our mid-summer Minneapolis heat and humidity. Good sports, the students bring snacks to share as we all root for each other in this sprint of a course.

Breaktime over, I face the class to propose another ethical dilemma. "Let's take the example of your hair stylist, who wants to come to you for therapy because you already know so much about . . ." Suddenly, my jaw drops and the words freeze in my throat. The students, alarmed at my expression, swing around in their chairs to see what has incapacitated me. There, on the other side of the window, with its nose almost pressed against the glass, is a fox. Impervious to other students strolling several yards away on campus, the fox locks eyes with me in a timeless moment.

Just then a student shrieks.

"It's the urine! It's the urine!" she cries, referring

to her latest gardening ploy to repel rabbits by using fox urine. "I must have tracked urine from my garden!" At that, the fox turns and scampers away as we all rush to the window for one last glimpse of the bushy tail.

Hmm, I wonder, *should I tell the class about the highly personal significance of foxes to me, or—especially in this ethics course—would that be too much information?*

Foxes had never really been on my radar, other than fairytales and nature specials on cable. But they kept "visiting" me in ways that got my attention. There was the classroom visit and also an appearance in the midst of a winter snowfall during a therapy session with a depressed adolescent. We were midway through our session, the busy highway outside my window having grown quiet, when a sudden movement caught my attention, my mouth agape.

"What is it?" the girl cried, afraid she'd revealed something alarming.

"Look out the window! It's a fox!"

And there, crossing a normally packed four-lane artery, a fox majestically sauntered across the highway as if she were greeting her subjects, her regal red fur richly contrasted against the white snow. We were transfixed. She was coming our way. Every moment, I thought a car would approach, but it was eerily quiet. Closer she ambled, between the trees, directly into the parking lot under my window, our eyes following her until she disappeared from view somewhere beneath us. Our interrupted therapy session took a totally different direction then, for the positive as I remember.

The fascination with foxes snuck up on me at an unassuming time in our lives when we decided to look at property to build a house. Initially thrilled at the hunt, I wearied a month into our search of exploring new subdivisions, tromping over frozen lots, and finishing the day disappointed. Just at that point, however, our realtor called for us to meet him at a site newly opened. We filled our water bottles—who knew house hunting could create such thirst?—and headed out.

We arrived to see John standing on a mound of dirt, smiling at us. Climbing to meet him, we stopped dead in our tracks at the view: a large wetland pond, geese, egrets, and herons. John informed us we were looking at Department-of-Natural-Resources-protected property, so no one could ever build behind us. *Oh, this could be it,* I thought as my heart quickened. I glanced at Reuel, who smiled at me. I could tell he was thinking the same thing.

Since a few lots were available, we narrowed our choice to two, right next to each other, and spent the next hour racing down one mound of dirt and up another, trying to calculate which would have the better view from the imagined living room. Each one had certain advantages over the other, and soon fatigue swamped us with the enormity of the decision. I turned to get the water bottles from the car as Reuel sat on a boulder in the middle of the first lot.

"This is it!" he cried, startling John and me. "If we can keep this boulder, this is the lot."

John laughed. "I'm sure the builders will be happy to not have to haul it away."

We made a deposit on the property, then spent the next several days agonizing about how much house we could afford to build. Every interaction between us seemed to start with, "Yes, but . . ."

"Yes, but with a main floor bedroom your mother could someday come live with us."

"Yes, but will we be house rich and cash poor? Will we still get to travel?"

"Yes, but we may only have this opportunity once."

"Yes, but . . ." And then it hit us. We were doing exactly what we taught our client couples to not do. Every time you respond to your partner with "Yes, but . . ." we endlessly explained to clients, it totally cancels out what the other just said. We even gave the dynamic a label— "But Monkeys." We challenged couples to keep the "But Monkeys" out of the dialogue and out of the marriage, but there we were, our conversation overrun with But Monkeys.

We started to chuckle, which then turned into full-on laughter as we simultaneously pointed at each other and accused, "But-Monkeys!"

"If our clients could see us now, they would think we're complete frauds," Reuel said, and we hooted and hollered even more. "Whoo," he said as he took a breath, "ya think we may have needed some comic relief?"

Somehow, in the next few days we decided on a house plan, held our collective breath, and signed the dotted line on the biggest financial commitment we had ever made. What a relief to have made a decision and mobilize around our direction! As our realtor predicted, the builders were pleased to not have to remove the monstrous boulder from the property, and later described how they "rolled" it from the foundation line down to the property edge by the pond, almost capsizing the backhoe in the process.

We quickly established a routine of heading to the site after work on Friday afternoons to see the progress of the building and absorb the new atmosphere. Sometimes we took Mountain Dew and brownies to the construction crew, sometimes we packed a picnic dinner and found a perch to eat our sandwiches.

One night during our June tornado season, a storm ripped through, dumping vast amounts of rain in what mom used to call a "gully washer." We somehow managed to get some sleep, but the next day we could hardly wait to get to the property to check for damage. The foundation was just poured a day or two earlier, so our drive to the site was tense, wondering if the foundation held or if the new walls had melted with the downpour. There! We jumped out of the car and raced to the lot where everything looked just like it should: the walls were solid, the sub-floor was still on, and nothing appeared ravished from the storm. We exhaled. I inhaled the pond view while Reuel traipsed down the hill to explore the pond's edge.

"Judy, come here!" he called.

Shoot. (My language, including the way I spoke in my own head, was still fairly wholesome at that stage of my life.) "Do I need to? Can I talk from here?" I looked at the weeds and stickers between us.

"You need to come here and see something."

I gingerly made my way to where he was standing beside the big repositioned boulder. "Do you see anything?" he asked.

I looked around, looked at the boulder, then abruptly saw what he meant. It looked like someone had taken a wide black Sharpie and made swirls on our rock. I was about to protest when Reuel directed me, "Look closer. What do you see?"

I zoomed out my focus and suddenly saw the profile outline of a fox, complete with shadings on the head, a darkened eye, and graceful snout.

"How did it get there?" I marveled.

Reuel took some time before he answered. "I think this was a sacred stone to the indigenous people, used in worship. I didn't tell you at the time, but remember when we were deciding between lots and I sat on this boulder? As soon as I put my hands on this rock I felt energy coming from it. That's why I knew this lot was the one, and why we needed to keep the boulder."

I absorbed that, surprised he hadn't mentioned his experience. "But why haven't we seen it before now?"

"I think this fox image was probably face down when it was up where the foundation is now poured. Then when the builders rolled it down here, it probably landed this side up. It took the storm last night to clear all the embedded dirt and debris out of the crevices so the fox image could emerge," he explained.

We stood awestruck before the boulder. I imagined its history and the people whose lives unfolded in the presence of this sacred stone. Did the indigenous people sense the energy emanating from the rock? Or was it the reverse, did their sacred rituals help to infuse it with energy? And how intense must that infusion of energy have been for us to notice it, even as I struggled with the creeping awareness that there were decades of abuse to those original people who were likely driven from this land. Sometimes awareness and truth were burdensome. I offered my thoughts as an inadequate acknowledgement to those elders, with a promise to respect their sacred stone. I closed my eyes and breathed.

I felt inexplicably connected to Reuel, to Spirit, and to the progression of people through the generations who sensed Spirit. Right there, amidst the weeds and burrs clinging to our clothes, listening to the great blue herons squawk their territorial claims, we felt that connection. It was exquisitely intimate and reassuringly communal.

After a few moments we looked at each other, not sure how to move on from there, when Reuel offered an impromptu benediction:

"The Divine is generous!"

The fox stone became a central focus of our backyard landscape. Fox continued to come to me in noticeable ways, each time driving my curiosity further to explore what such appearances might mean. Nothing in my fundamentalist background had prepared me for this, so a friend loaned his guide to animal spirits. According to the author, a Seneca elder of the Wolf Clan, Fox is a messenger of danger, sickness, or possible death but is also a good power and guardian. In fact, certain shamans can use the power and spirit of clever and loyal Fox to reverse a problem, like bringing someone out of a coma.

I dropped the book. *Are you kidding about death? Or a coma? Forget that!* Nobody was going to die on my watch. But the part about reversing a problem compelled me. We could maybe use some of that power—who wouldn't want to reverse a problem! I wondered if the problem had to be as serious as a coma, or if I had to become a shaman in order to change things.

Reversing a problem or illness, I knew from my clients, exacts a painful price before it brings relief. I also knew it on a personal level, I realized, as I thought about the time several years before when I had to stand up to Reuel about treatment for my thyroid cancer. Our relationship almost sunk into a coma before our chilly marital condition reversed.

18
Trust Again

"Struggling is always worthwhile when the end point is a breakthrough into a deeper and more meaningful experience of life."
—Chelsea Wakefield

Early March

For almost three weeks now, Reuel's mind has been at the mercy of medications. The whiplash from the gentle, heart-filled moments to the stunned states of "what-did-he-just-say?" strains our emotional muscles. In the space of a few minutes, we careen from the sublime to the ridiculous to the realistic. One day, watching a romantic movie scene between two lovers, Reuel smiles and brings my hand to his lips. Then the nurse enters to let him know she is getting his next dose of medication.

Reuel replies, "Let me know if you have any trouble. I'll contact the mafia." She leaves trying to suppress a smile, and he turns to me. "This would be interesting about the brain if it wasn't me or my family."

We begin to fear something more than medication is amiss with his brain. The radiation has decreased his pain level, so the dosage of narcotics has been decreased. But his mind has not likewise recovered. This morning, the oncologist orders a brain scan. My own brain halts as the implications engulf me: metastasis to the brain!

The transport aide arrives and invites me along on the field trip to the MRI unit. Reuel is cheerful, as always, to everyone he encounters, joking about their duties or the weather, happily oblivious to the potential diagnosis. I feel stark terror at the chance he may have brain cancer.

"You can wait here, Mrs. Tiesel." The aide points at a small waiting area. "I'll take your husband back for his scan, and when he's done we'll be out to pick you up."

I nod as if he'd just dropped me at the grocery and was going to park the car. The family area holds four typical pleather and chrome waiting-room chairs and a couple of tables with lamps. My body seeks the chair with the table closest to it. I set down my coffee cup and pull out my ubiquitous paperback for just such a time. I can't read. My ears are keened to hear Reuel's voice or name. Nothing. It must be the quietest cubby in the whole hospital.

My watch shows only five minutes have passed. The aide said it wouldn't take long. How long is not long? These past five minutes are some of the longest of this whole ordeal.

I try closing my eyes and praying, but my mind flashes through every reference to brain cancer I can remember, clear back to my second year of marriage when I worked for a surgeon. The patients had changed markedly from one visit to the next. Acquaintances whose family members had brain cancer confided the agonizing progressive debilitation of their relatives and their relationships as they lost their loved ones in slow motion.

Dear God—there's my prayer—is this the next phase of the journey for us? Do we have to witness his mind disintegrating? When is this nightmare going to end so we can get Reuel back?

Just then, they wheel him out of the imaging room. Reuel looks into my eyes.

"Are you okay?" he asks.

"Oh, I'm just tired."

He looks at me with concern. "I know this must be hard for you."

Huh? *In spite of his pain, the narcotics, and his new home of the hospital, he notices something amiss with me. I feel treasured. Then I feel utterly desolated at the thought of brain cancer ripping him away, and right now he has no idea what might be occurring within him. Does anyone?*

Inside Look: Counseling Office, Mid-Career

"What do you mean I've had trauma? I have *never* been sexually abused!"

Delores was referred to me by a colleague who was doing marital therapy with her and her husband. He described how on multiple occasions they seemed to have a breakthrough one week, only to be back in the same stuck spot the next week. He suspected there might be trauma in her background. Judging by the depth of her reaction just now, I tend to agree with my colleague.

"You may be absolutely right, Delores. Let's just pause and take a few big, deep breaths . . . that's right. What do you notice now?"

"I feel calmer. My heart isn't beating so fast, and I don't feel so scared."

"That's good, I'm glad you're feeling calmer. Do you know what happened that got you so scared?"

"Well, when you said trauma, that would be the worst thing that could ever happen to anyone. I couldn't stand that! What does that even mean?" Her breathing accelerates even as the color drains from her face.

"It's a good question, but first let's check our breathing. Good breaths, blowing out all the way . . . And what are you noticing in your feet?" (When clients' fears get triggered, it often helps to draw their attention to a part of the body—like the feet—that helps to ground them in the present.)

"Yes, Delores, I can see your toes wiggle. That's great. Do you feel ready to go on? Okay, may I go back to your question about trauma?" She nods. "You can stop me whenever you need." I take my own deep breath and wiggle my own toes as I shift into helping her understand.

"With all the examples we hear in the media, our understanding of trauma can be confusing. Very simply, trauma is what happens when our brain gets overwhelmed with incoming data. For example, if you were in a car accident, there's all kinds of information for your brain to suddenly and immediately process: Where am I? Am I okay? Do I need help? How bad is the car? Is anyone else hurt?

"When the brain gets overwhelmed, it doesn't know where to 'file' the data, so the data gets stuck. And if it doesn't ever get processed or filed correctly, it stays stuck. Then, without us realizing it, that unprocessed data pops up at unexpected times. It may pop up and feel like anything from confusion and forgetfulness to a panic attack to 'checking out.' Does that make sense?"

"I think so," she responds slowly, "but my brain may be overwhelmed right now! What if I really do have trauma?"

"If you do, then there's a wonderful technique called EMDR that helps file all that disorganized data into its proper places."

"Foxstone," our enjoyably pretentious nickname for our new building site, slowly took shape. Friends had warned us what a headache it could be, building a home. It turned out the headache became quite literal for Reuel. As the process of construction intensified, so did his headaches. At the housing site, contractors examined the jobs, plumbed, wired, drywalled, mudded, and sanded. At various medical sites, specialists examined, palpated, X-rayed, imaged, and consulted Reuel. They took endless histories to glean something that would ease the pain. Finally, we went together to a consultation with the last of the specialists, a neurosurgeon. He asked routine questions, which must have been recorded in his chart five times over. Then he gave us his diagnosis.

"We have found nothing organic from all the testing you've been through. In that case, the pain must be psychological," he stated flatly.

I leapt out of the chair, headed straight for the exit, hissing about the mandate to practice in one's area of competence and fuming at the doctor's arrogance. By the time Reuel caught up to me in the parking lot, I was still steaming. His whole body slumped.

"I'll do anything," he said. "This pain is real, whatever it comes from, and if it's psychological then I need to treat that."

His desperation tore through me. My mind flashed to a member of my consultation group who had reported good results—physical and emotional—with a specific technique for trauma called EMDR (Eye Movement Desensitization and Reprocessing).

"Give me her number," Reuel said, when I told him about it. "Something's got to change."

It did change. It got worse. He had just begun the process of EMDR when the stress in our marriage grew in proportion to the progress on the new house. Reuel, who had always gone silent when he was displeased, was now irritable. At me. A lot. He spoke in clipped sentences. I asked what was wrong. He gave vague answers. He eventually told me he was encountering intense, painful childhood history in his therapy, so I indulged his unfamiliar irritation, feeling rather generous.

Over that summer, he continued in therapy, the builders continued on the new house, and I continued to ready our old house for selling. A few months earlier, when we were targeting the date to put the house on the market, I had told Reuel that my thirtieth high school reunion in Walla Walla was scheduled right around when we might be ready to show our house. Reuel had said he thought he could handle that by himself, along with the realtor, as long as everything was pretty much set up. He didn't want me to miss the reunion.

So all summer, in spare moments, I sorted, packed, de-cluttered, and scoured every room in the house, until the garage was full of boxes, closets were spacious, and the laundry room was spotless. I periodically gave Reuel progress reports about the state of the house, checked with him when I made airline reservations, and shared my excitement about seeing old friends at the reunion.

He was quiet as he took me to the airport. I realized that he hadn't been as excited for me as usual and that he was probably unhappy about something. But by that time I didn't really care. He had been unhappy a lot, and I knew I had done my part to get the house ready.

My mother picked me up at the airport, and it wasn't five

minutes after walking through the front door to her house that Reuel's first call came.

"Is something wrong with the house or the construction?" she
asked.

"No, he was just checking on some items," I told her. He
called frequently at shorter intervals. "Now something else is going
on. . . ." I said, not wanting to tell my mom how angry and blaming
he sounded.

When I was getting ready for the big event of the weekend,
the phone rang yet again. I was tempted to not answer, but my mother picked up and then called to me to pick up.

"Hello."

"Hi." Long pause.

"I'm in the middle of getting dressed here . . ."

And then he let it rip. "How could you do this to me?!" he
shouted.

"What are you talking about? What did I do?"

"If I had done this to you . . ." he trailed off.

"What is it I have done to you?" I was more confused than
upset. Strangely, I was not feeling responsible for him and was not
rushing to make him feel better.

"You have left me all alone, totally responsible for selling this
house. I would never have done this to you! And I'm going through
my own pain, processing my stuff in this EMDR. I just can't believe
you'd do this!" His words spilled out, as angry as I'd ever heard him.

"If you remember, we planned and agreed to this at the beginning of summer. You even suggested it." I was amazingly calm,
hoping logic would get through to him.

"Damn you, how can you do this?"

I gasped. We had never even told each other to shut up, let

alone sworn at the other. What the hell was happening? I scrambled to make sense of it. Yes, he had been going through a tough time in his therapy. No, he had not been totally himself. But why was he taking it out on me? My mind raced to understand.

Wham! The first realization hit: He had not yet asked me for anything but was already blaming me for not giving it.

After the many stories I heard about his childhood, I knew it was difficult for him to ask for things, so I tried to help him out. *Aaagh*, I thought with a thud, *maybe I have enabled him*. Hadn't I always tried to anticipate what he needed? Yes, like quiet time to himself, the comfort of making love, finding time to talk to the kids about some frustration. He knew how to convey the message. I knew how to decode it. I protected him from having to ask.

No more! Sitting there on the other end of that phone connection, I was done with the old pattern. I was no longer going to provide solutions. He would have to ask for what he needed. My level of self-trust and resolve was amazing! And it lasted for three seconds.

Wham! My hands went clammy and my stomach started to churn. The second realization hit: I was terrified!

In nano-seconds my mind ricocheted potential reasons for my fear, all focused on questions about Reuel. Was I somehow pushing him past his limits of stability? Was he strong enough to ask for what he needed? Would he collapse in shame, believing he was deficient? Or would he punish me by withdrawing his presence? Never speak to me again? And finally, would this change in our pattern be worth the inner turmoil and potential new problems it could create?

Reuel was quiet on the other end of the line. The pressure inside me mounted to respond to him, but the confusion in my head needed to clear before I trusted myself to speak. Some of this emotional and mental chaos, I realized, felt familiar.

Wham! The third realization hit: I dreaded he would end up being like my father. Unacceptable. I refused to be stuck living with the kind of person from whom I had escaped almost three decades ago. Then from the turmoil of my dismay a single question began to crystallize: Was Reuel so weak that I had to protect him? My doubt was so painful that I slid to the floor, curling up around my heartache.

And that was the moment I knew I had to trust him and myself in a wholly deeper way. I chose to trust my truth and Reuel's strength to ask one simple but pivotal question, one I knew he dreaded.

"What is it you want?" I asked softly.

I heard the gasp over the phone line. "You *know* how difficult it is for me to ask for things," his voice filled with betrayal and anger.

Somehow I kept quiet, this time not because I was afraid to speak but because I believed my integrity—and his—were at stake. After several moments of tense silence, he spoke in a tight, staccato voice. "Would. You. Please. Come. Back?"

"Yes. I'll find out when the next flight leaves."

We hung up. I went to the reunion that night with my gut aching as if I'd done a hundred abdominal crunches. I had exercised new trust muscles and was exhausted. I flew out the next morning, leaving a confused mother and not knowing how Reuel would greet me at the airport.

I don't know if I ever told him how difficult that crossroads was for me. It would have been so easy to give in and say by my actions, "Of course, it's difficult for you to ask, so you don't have to. I'll jump in and do it anyway." But I knew deep in my spirit that he needed to ask. I wanted him to trust me enough to ask. I also knew that I needed to not rescue him. I needed to trust him to not morph into his dad or mine. We each needed to grow and trust in order to change our pattern and deepen our marriage.

Reuel and I learned over the years, and taught the couples we worked with, that ultimately trust is a decision. We either decide to trust, or we decide not to. If we decide not to trust, it won't matter how much a spouse does to "earn" that trust. But if we can have the courage to risk even a modicum of trust, the course of a marriage might be altered.

By staying with my truth that summer, by trusting Reuel to turn toward me instead of away, I was inadvertently inviting us both to a deeper level of knowledge. I risked knowing I could withstand my own angst while waiting for him to ask for what he needed. He risked being known as someone who had a need, trusting I wouldn't repeat the patterns of his parents. Although we didn't feel it at the time, the risks we took established roots at a deeper level of intimacy. We would come to rely on the depth and breadth of those roots to anchor us.

19
Balancing Between

"Committed relationships force each of us to develop integrity—
or to flee from it—in the context of being connected to someone
we care about. . . . In your partnership, integrity is mostly about
confronting *yourself*. It pushes you up against your own fears,
issues, and limitations, and challenges you to deal with them."
—Resmaa Menakem

Early March

*At the start of this third week of hospitalization, Reuel is still in a
constant state of mental confusion. The doctors have finally managed
the narcotics dosage for pain, but they just discovered he has hypocal-
caemia, low calcium levels in the blood, which has the same effect of
confusion as overmedication. This time, though, Reuel appears to be
withdrawing into himself. He is listless when I walk into the room,
he has no appetite, and his eyes are dull. I am alarmed in a whole new
way at seeing the energy dissipate from this larger-than-life man.
Even with pain and narcotics, he had been vibrant.*

*My heart pounds as I watch him, and I feel torn. Two op-
posing forces are gathering momentum within me. In one corner is
the drive to will Reuel into health for his sake and mine. I just can't
imagine life without him. And in the other corner, unexpected, is the*

drive to let him go, so he won't suffer any more physical pain or the anguish of drug-induced delusions. I don't know which side to take.

My stomach has become the battleground where the force of "He must live" meets the force of "He must not suffer." How can a winner possibly emerge? We're doomed. No. My mind will not go there. I know he will gain the victory. Wounded, perhaps, but victorious. Don't we have some divine assurance about that? But now we have to contend with the hypercalcaemia. I am suddenly overcome with battle fatigue.

Dear God, *I breathe*, how much more? *I pick up my tablet and start to pray through my pen.*

Lord, I don't like to ask for things much, at least not so directly. I ask Reuel for things, because I trust him. Do I not trust you? Ah, trust vs. guarantee.

I'm embarrassed at how I don't trust. Please search my spirit. I don't want Reuel to die — not for me, nor for our kids, nor for all the people he has impacted and will impact. I know there's selfishness in my request. But out of my heart, full of love, I ask.

I ask for you to halt the lymphoma. Please let his body have a chance to regroup so he can fight it the way you designed him. Forgive my fear in asking. I don't want to be disappointed. I want to trust. I will. I decide to trust. I trust you even as my gut clenches. Even knowing trust is a decision I learned from Reuel.

Humbly, I ask, and I trust. Yeah, I know, there are no guarantees in trust. Amen.

I look up from the journal, and there on the television screen sweeps a bald eagle. I desperately want to believe it is a sign my prayer has been answered, that the healing has already begun.

A few minutes later the chaplain stops by and Reuel rouses. Reuel has described his engaging and stimulating discussions with Chaplain Ann during previous hospital admits, and I'm happy to finally meet her. As she enters the room, Reuel tells her, "The bear was chased away. Judy and I fought it. It was scary, but it was okay."

I look to the chaplain, who glances at me. She may have read my thoughts: Huh? More delusions?

He makes a remark I don't quite catch, except for the words, "in the spirit." She agrees and notes how his spiritual muscles and depth have served him well. Then she turns to me and tells of an incident last week when his nurse was concerned whether he had enough pain medication to bridge the withdrawal from the Fentanyl patch. Ann said she would pray as the bridge. Her prayers could be the transition to ease into the new medication. His face relaxed, and she thought he was in the spirit then.

I am struck by the fact I had not heard this story before now. It's the kind of experience Reuel has taken delight in sharing because it's another example of the Divine's presence. But Reuel wasn't able to keep the experience in his head long enough to be able to retell it. So much of his essence is clouded. Will we ever get him back?

Ann asks if she can pray with us, and we huddle beside the bed, my one hand on Reuel's arm, the other in Ann's hand. I momentarily rest in her strength. I don't have to be strong for her. She prays for the Spirit to fill this room and for Reuel to receive all that the Divine has for him. Her prayer ends. I am filled. I look at Reuel and want to believe his eyes don't seem quite as far away.

 Inside Look: Supervision Group of MFT Practica Students, Mid-Career

My supervision group of six students is full of enthusiasm and a bit of anxiety as we gather for our twice-monthly meetings. They are placed in different agencies around the metro in order to get hands-on experience of being therapists. It's my job as a faculty supervisor to give guidance they can use in their therapy sessions and to help them avoid ethical mistakes.

"Okay, who has a case to present today? Shannon? Good, go ahead and give us some background details," I begin.

Shannon shares, "I have this couple who are as old as my parents, and they are having problems with their son, who is my age. I don't think I can work with them, because it's like I'd be working with my parents!"

"Oh no, anything but that!" I teased as the group laughed. "What do the parents say is the problem?"

"Their son has moved back home because of finances, but they say he won't help out with keeping things cleaned up, and his girlfriend stays until super late, sometimes overnight. They think they've smelled marijuana coming from his room, and they feel generally disrespected. They thought they were done with parenting when he left home for college."

I observed this group whose ages ranged from mid-twenties—looking now a bit awkward—to midlife. "Parenting has changed over the past few years, and many parents now say that parenting their adult children is the hardest stage of all, even worse than the terrible twos or the teenage years." The midlife students relaxed into their chairs, a smile of recognition across their faces as I explained further. "We know now that the brain doesn't fully mature until about twenty-five years, which together with expectations for college or further training means that adolescence is extended. But most adolescents believe that once they hit age eighteen or twenty-one, they should be treated like adults. So these two ways of thinking inevitably clash, and then the parents end up in your counseling office to get help."

"But how do I help them?" Shannon wailed.

"Balance. You not only have to balance your own reactions about how close the client's situation is to your own life, but you have to help the clients find a new balance between respecting their adult child and respecting themselves."

....

Balancing between two opposing forces can pretty much sum up parenting, especially parenting kids who are college-age and beyond. One force pushes us to let go, while the other force clings to them because they're "not ready" to be so independent. I usually see moms having more trouble with seeing their kids ready to be on their own, which may reflect a mom's feeling about the job she has done as a parent. Dads, I've noticed, tend to focus on how their kids can support themselves or how much financial support from the family will be required, which also may reflect a dad's feelings about his role as provider, even when he's not the main breadwinner.

This whole process of launching our kids is like walking a balance beam. Not only do we have to step carefully with precision posture, but once we believe we've got the balance down, the beam changes and we have to regain a whole new equilibrium. And it's not just the launching (or launched) child which tests our balance, but so does the marriage. Our intimate other is right up there on the balance beam with us! What one does to stabilize themselves ripples in its impact to the equilibrium of the other. Balancing, in this progression of launching and relating to your adult child, requires both hanging on and letting go at the same time.

I thought my balance was pretty good by the time our third child, Cory, reached adulthood. We'd had his brother and sister to practice on by the time Cory was in his twenties, but my poise plunged the first time he brought his significant partner home. I liked Amanda, it's not that I didn't, but she was eight years older than Cory and had an entirely different life agenda. Except she pretended she didn't, which activated my trust alarms. To be fair to her, though, she got points from me for changing her career plans to transfer to New Jersey, where she supported Cory in his quest to act on Broadway. I was pleased when they called to tell us they were coming, but their approaching visit raised a concern, one I thought I better run by Reuel soon after we hung up from talking with them.

Reuel bounced in from the other room. "Isn't it great they're coming to stay with us in another couple of weeks?"

"Absolutely!" I nodded. Inside, I was hesitating to say this next part, and wondered about that, but proceeded anyway. "And I'll let them decide which one sleeps in the upstairs bedroom, and which one downstairs."

Reuel stopped in his tracks to look at me. "What? Why?

They're already living together, for God's sake!"

I flinched. That hurt. There was judgement in his words. "Yes, but this is our house, and we should be able to live our values in our house."

"Just what are those values you want to communicate?"

"Well I don't want to communicate all the 'living in sin' baggage from the church. But Cory knows what we've always believed about living together before marriage, or at least before engagement—that it can prematurely stunt the couple's growth. That it's not ideal, spiritually, for their relationship. What does that communicate to him if we throw away those beliefs?" I noticed my voice had risen, along with my heart rate.

Reuel's phone rang just then. I was grateful for the interruption. I went upstairs to work on my schedule for the rest of the week, or at least that was my cover story, since my focus was off. I was confused, hurt, and trying to still this cyclone within my chest. After all the conversations we have had through the years, how could Reuel now be positioned so totally opposite of what we've always talked about? I thought we were united in our values, and it was painful to realize we were not. I squeezed my eyes shut, but a tear or two escaped. I knew we were not done talking, but I wanted a break before I reentered the disagreement.

A couple of days later, we were back into it.

"I don't understand what you're trying to do, with putting them in separate bedrooms. Do you think they aren't sexual in New York?" Reuel's tone was slightly less accusing than before.

"I know they are, but that's not my house. That's theirs."

"And don't we want them to be welcome here?"

Argh! "Of course, but does that mean we drop our values to make them feel better?"

"Do you hear what you're saying? What's the point of two bedrooms except to communicate judgement to them?"

I took a deep breath and tried to slow my anger and confusion, but Reuel jumped in before I had a chance to respond.

"Look how many of your friends live together or have lived together before they were married. Would you make them sleep in separate bedrooms if they stayed with us? Do you judge them?"

"No, I wouldn't, and no, I don't!"

"So what's the difference?"

"They're not my child!"

Reuel frowned, and I could see he was feeling intensely—some anger, but something else I couldn't identify from his expression. Was he judging me for sticking to what used to be "our" values? When did he change? Why didn't he tell me?

Plus, and I felt petty-minded about this realization, it seemed like Cory's feelings were more important to Reuel than my feelings. That rattled me. Reuel was supposed to prefer me over the kids. I tried again to make him see my point.

"Look, whenever I'm counseling parents of adult kids and this topic comes up, I have always encouraged them to honor their own values in their own house. I have always believed that's been the best counsel. But what you're saying is opposite that!" My voice was higher, and I sounded a bit desperate.

Have I been wrong all these years? Have I given bad advice?

No, I didn't believe that, I thought to myself, because being wrong or giving bad advice would have set off my internal "unbalanced load" buzzer. Then I would have rebalanced the load by redistributing or removing the dogmatic or inflexible pieces. But then again, I was feeling uneasy and wondered if I had ignored the buzzer regarding the bedrooms. What were my options here—a rigid bedroom fundamentalist or a flexible hypocrite?

My mind flashed to a time when I was snorkeling in Grand Cayman and got so involved watching the brilliant undersea world that when I raised my head to wave to my family in the cove, I didn't know where I was. The cove and my family had disappeared! And I didn't know which way to swim to return to them.

No wonder that scene came to mind. Like the bedroom dilemma, I was unsure about my direction, suddenly in unchartered territory. How could I hang onto myself and not give up? I was scared in that Caribbean Sea, afraid I would make a decision that would take me even farther from my family. There was only one decision that made sense to me then, and that was to swim to the nearest beach house and ask directions. By the time I pulled myself ashore and brushed some of the sand off, I caught a flash of neon orange out of the corner of my left eye. It was Marci's swimsuit! There was the cove! There was my family, right where I had inadvertently swam away from them. Once I knew which direction to take, I got back in the water and swam until I again entered the cove.

But what that scene meant to me as I was considering my options was not so specific. Like then, I was scared I would make a decision that would take me further away from those I love. I was trying to hang onto myself and honor my integrity, but I didn't see anyone around that I could ask for directions. Perhaps I needed to keep going with what I knew until some flash of neon-colored insight directed me otherwise.

Reuel was waiting, watching me. There had been enough of a pause in our conversation as I recalled that scene that some of the intensity had drained from each of us, so I continued explaining to him.

"I want to honor my integrity here. I want to make a decision out of that integrity, not out of my anxiety about how you or Cory will react."

He nodded. His face relaxed. I saw he really heard me, and that helped. He took a breath and exhaled deeply. "My concern is that the values you're holding onto will interfere with your or our relationship with Cory."

I should have kept my mouth shut there, but I didn't. "Are you saying we have to do what Cory wants in order to keep the relationship? How is that healthy?"

Reuel tossed his hands in the air like he'd given up and said he needed to get things ready for work tomorrow. *Well then! Evidently we are done talking for the night!* I didn't quite stomp off, but it was close.

We walked around this relational pothole for several days, but Cory's approaching visit loomed closer. Reuel was first to broach the subject.

"Have you been thinking any more about the bedroom situation when Cory and Amanda come?"

"Yeah, I have. And of course I have a new client couple dealing with these same kinds of issues with their adult kids."

"Of course!" Relieved, we laughed together at how it

always seemed to happen that our clients' issues tended to present when we were dealing with the very same thing in our personal lives. "And . . . ?"

"I'd like to say I've had some brilliant insight to resolve it all, but I haven't. I think a lot about your concern over the relationship with Cory, and the last thing I want is to damage it. He and I just repaired some of the damage from his high school days. But I can't—or should I say don't want to—swallow my convictions. I spent too many years doing that in order to please my parents, or some boss, or some board member." I stopped abruptly. Shit, I hoped he wouldn't ask if he was included in that list of who I try to please. I wasn't ready to go there.

"What are you going to do?"

I had no answer to that.

Two nights before Cory's arrival, I was having fitful sleep. The question must have been flooding my unconscious, because as I worked my way back to bed from the bathroom at 4 a.m., I blurted a prayer, "What should I do?"

Immediately I received an understanding. *Let it go*, was my internal answer.

Really? But . . .

Let it go. The relationship is everything.

Ooof, right in the gut. That, then, was my flash of neon-colored insight. I leaned against the wall from the sudden breathlessness, which eliminated the need for me to ask if this was real. After a few moments, peace filled me.

Instead of feeling like I had compromised my convictions, I felt like I had direction. I got it, then. My value of "separate-but-equal-bedrooms" was no longer adequate. Instead,

a greater, more essential value was required, one of relationship. I internally checked around to see how my integrity was
faring. Fine! Integrity was honored, because this decision was
now all mine, arriving there with my own insights and understandings. I finally had a way to swim back to my family.

An invitation to intimacy doesn't always look like one.
In this situation, I had to become fully known to myself and
recognize my own integrity before I could be known to or by
Reuel. Years later, I shared this story with Cory, which ended up being an inadvertent invitation to intimacy. That is, he
now knows his dad, me, and our marriage more fully, and his
responses helped me better know him.

20
Surprises

Early March

It's an American Idol *night, and I'm seeing a client late at the office. Marci left me a message that she was able to get off work early so she could be with her dad. When I finally arrive, she pulls me aside to catch me up on what she has observed.*

Looking into my eyes with concern, Marci says, "Mom, I was really delighted at how playful dad was when I got here. He was chewing on his straw, chatting with that volunteer who gives him hand massages, and then we all bantered. Really, it was the best I've seen him in a while. When the volunteer finished packing up her lotions and leaving, she called out, 'I'll see you tomorrow.'

"Then dad looked over at me and said, 'Won't she be surprised tomorrow.' I asked him about what, but he kind of made fun of me. He said, 'You know.' I thought it was another one of his 'crazy daddy' moments.

"But then he said, 'I have to write out a death notice.' I wasn't sure what he meant, so I asked if he meant a will, a death notice like a will. He said, 'Yes, because I am going to die tomorrow.'"

"What?" I half-ask. I'm appalled, but I want to be strong for Marci. "Oh, how awful for you. What did you do?"

"I took a big breath and said, 'No, you're not going to die tomorrow, not for many years from now.' He asked me if I was kidding, then he started to cry. He warned me not to joke about something like this."

"How did you respond to that?" I ask.

"That's when I jumped up to rub his arm and head. I told him I'd never joke about his dying."

"And is that the point when I entered the scene?" She nods yes, tears in her eyes.

I turn to Reuel, who has been watching us, and cup his face with my hands. "I'm so sorry. What a strange experience for you."

"I just have to let in that I won't be dying tomorrow," he says, as if he can't quite believe it. He looks to me on one side of the bed and to Marci on the other side for confirmation.

"That's right," we say simultaneously. I wonder if Marci has a small bubble of doubt like I do.

He stretches a hand to each of us, and we hold on as we all cry, at his pain and relief, our own pain and relief, at this arduous journey we're on, and maybe at the modicum of doubt that can't be entirely erased.

Suddenly Reuel starts frantically wresting the sheet up higher and higher. We are instantly sober, watching him intently, ready to call the nurse to ease the pain that must be coming. Then, abruptly, he stops pulling. Instead, he uses the sheet to dry his tears. Marci and I burst into laughter. It's another punctuation of the absurd.

Later Marci makes a note in our hospital room journal, the place where she and I keep track of blood tests, the doctor's reports, questions we want to ask, and notes to each other. "The ability to laugh guilt-free at that is what makes us members in this sacred and strange caregivers club . . . I wonder what tomorrow will actually bring."

He doesn't die that next day. But now I realize that energies were beginning to shift within him, and he was accessing a deep knowledge about his remaining time with us.

Inside Look: Office, Late Career

My caseload had been too full to see any premarital couples for quite a few years, but a space opened in my schedule to see a couple recommended by a pastor friend. I wondered why she was not conducting her usual counsel-before-wedding procedure for the twenty-something couple in her church.

"Well," she said, "this is more like a forty-or-fifty-something couple. They've been previously married, and they each have their own kids. It seemed like there were too many surprises with them for me to feel comfortable with the usual premarital counseling. Uh . . . good luck."

When I walked into the waiting room to meet Stan and Serena, they seemed excited to be there and eager to learn. I gathered the routine background information without any red flags emerging until I asked about their previous marriages. Serena shrank into the couch while Stan got big.

"All of that is in the past," he stated in a raised voice. "We've been forgiven by our Lord for failing at marriage, and that's a closed book. We're moving on." Hmm. That's the therapist equivalent of "Sick-em" to a trained-to-fight pit bull, but I knew I wouldn't get any more information by directly challenging him.

"We can come back to that, but I'd be curious to know what you learned about yourself from your first marriage."

"I learned everything I needed to marry this beautiful woman who makes me so happy," he replied in a case-closed kind of way.

"And for you, Serena?"

"Well, I learned I don't like surprises." All of a sudden her voice got stronger. She sat forward and pushed her shoulders back. "My first husband threw me surprise birthday parties, and I hated them. They were excuses for him to drink with his buddies. Then he surprised me with a cruise to the Bahamas, but he charged so much on our credit card that it took years to pay off."

I noticed Stan began to slowly shrink the more Serena talked. "But honey . . ."

"Don't interrupt me, Stan! I need to say this right now if we have any hope of getting married." She turned to me, probably reading my surprise. "Sorry, Doc, but Stan has let one too many surprises drop. He just told me he has a son from when he got his high school girlfriend pregnant. Then he has been talking about being the leader in the family, like the Bible says. He wants my two teenage children to instantly obey him, no questions asked. But they don't even know him. And he doesn't know them!"

She paused, glanced at Stan, then stiffened her back even more. "Worst of all, last week he told me that if I don't submit to him sexually like a good wife, then he'll have no choice but to satisfy his needs elsewhere. And it would be my fault!"

I'm not sure which of the three of us was most surprised by her candor. But she wasn't finished.

"I've just realized by being here, and by you asking what I've learned about myself, that I don't want another marriage with those kinds of surprises. Good-bye, Stan." She gathered her things and walked out of the office.

Stan, stunned, turned to me. After a moment, his face reddened and he stood up, launching his pointed finger toward my face. "Doc, this is all your fault! You'll hear from my lawyer!"

Several years ago, there was a series of television commercials featuring a variety of weary travelers who were surprised by the lack of amenities in the hotel they had booked: extra charge for sheets, no bathroom in the room, or unwanted four-legged roommates. The next reservation, the shocked guests vowed, would be with the featured hotel, where "The best surprise is no surprise."

Maybe there are marriages in which no surprises ever happen, but I'm not sure I would consider that a good surprise—or a healthy marriage. If there are no surprises, is the defining factor of the relationship stagnation? What keeps the life-giving nutrients from stagnating if there is no fresh input of surprise? I don't mean a whole deluge of surprises in which one never knows what to expect, but the occasional surprise stirs the waters and keeps the relational system fresh, warding off the decay of boredom. That doesn't mean all surprises are wanted and pleasant, but even the unexpected visitor protects the pond population from stagnation.

Birthdays, holidays, anniversaries, and other rites of passage all hold the potential for surprises and stirring the relational waters. Reuel's fiftieth birthday, for example, when he requested to make love five times, surprised me, then in turn surprised him with how disregarded he felt, then came back to surprise me when he confronted me a year later. Neither of us would have labeled these as pleasant surprises, but they certainly kept us from getting bored! And provided a means for each of us to grow and eventually deepen our intimacy.

By the time our thirtieth anniversary arrived, I thought we agreed on how we wanted to celebrate. I wanted to give a party—not a surprise party—surrounded by friends and family who could share and celebrate the significance of a thirty-year union in which we still loved each other. We did that with an evening of music, toasts, and re-enacted cake cutting. The only surprises were two: first, a minor meltdown in the afternoon when Reuel and I disagreed about whether to set up tables or have people balance plates on their laps (tables, of course!), and second, the equal parts of laughter and tears during our friends' toasts. The latter was a much more welcome surprise than the former, but even the meltdown became an amusing part of the retelling.

Unknown to me, Reuel had a different celebration in mind. We took the kids to Sunday brunch the weekend before our anniversary party to enjoy a celebration with just the five of us and had just returned to the house when Reuel told us to wait by the fireplace. The kids, puzzled, looked at me, but

I shrugged my shoulders. Soon Reuel called us to the dining room to sit at our places, champagne flutes effervescing and a parchment scroll tied with a ribbon at each place.

"I want us to toast our success in marriage and as a family, and then I'll let you know when you can unroll the scrolls." He raised his glass. "To God, to love, and to growing together."

We responded with a series of crystal clinks as we repeated the phrase until every glass had been included, and then we drank to his heartfelt words.

"Wait, there's something in my glass!" Aaron cried. I caught Reuel stifling a smile.

"Mine too!" from another. At once the kids and I were draining the flutes to find what our treasures were. Finally Aaron saw what it was: a silver ring with a stone surrounded by gold markings. Then Marci got to her ring, which had a different stone but the same markings, and Cory's ring was yet a different stone. My eyes darted between Reuel and each of them.

Now it was my turn to shake the ring from the bottom of the glass. Yes, silver with the gold markings, but instead of a stone, there were five small diamonds. I looked at Reuel for an explanation.

"Ok, now you can open the scrolls," he said.

Dear Aaron, Marci, & Cory,

In many ways, you have been with us for all of the years we (your parents) have loved each other. Somehow, it also seems appropriate to mark this occasion with your own ring from this family. As we each continue to grow older and move in many directions, we nonetheless have always been, and will always be, family. The ring we want you to have is simply a reminder that wherever you go, whatever you do, near or far from this home, you always have been loved and always will be loved.

Your ring is a combination of several things, created from the love of this family and the love our families before us have shared. Grandma Tiesel gave us grandpa's wedding ring and Grandma Watson gave us a wedding ring from her side of the family. So the gleaming pieces of gold come from those wedding bands and have been melted into this new ring. The stone in your ring marks the time you entered our family. That moment was extremely special for us. This, too, is a special moment in our family's history.

I was as surprised as the kids about the rings and the scrolls, but he generously included me in the message to them, just as he included the children in the importance of our anniversary. He gave an exquisite surprise.

Looking back, I realize now how the timing of these gifts helped secure and tether us. We planned an autumn trip to continue our anniversary celebration, not knowing there was a most unwelcome surprise just ahead, one that was to stir the waters to a froth.

21
Crossroads

"Are you more willing to let yourself be highly vulnerable in
pursuit of deep intimacy, or are you more willing to sacrifice some
level of intimacy to avoid being highly vulnerable?"
—Eli J. Finkel

Early March

Another evening dissolves at the hospital, chatting together, watching a little television, monitoring Reuel's color and spirits, and gleaning whatever I can from medical personnel who walk into the room. As I gather my things to make the trip home, I pause with dread, considering the ten-minute solitary walk down the long, empty, echoing corridors of the hospital. It looms longer than the twenty-minute drive home.

Just before I leave, one of our favorite nurses comes to check on Reuel. She sees how tangled his bedding is, but in the course of fixing it, she triggers severe muscle spasms in his back. I drop my coat and bags, realizing this pain looks like a bad round. The mortified nurse orders pain relievers and muscle relaxants en masse, but it takes several hours for the muscles to cease their spasms. Do I stay with him, or go home? How many times have I pulled up to that intersection of choice in the last few weeks? I stay so he can rest easier.

After several minutes, Reuel jolts awake in fear. He whispers to me that his suspicions are centered on a particular staff member who "isn't to be trusted." I don't respond immediately. My dilemma is trying to sift through what is real. Reuel has always had a deep knowing about people and can sense very early after meeting them if they are trustworthy or if they are troubled in harmless or harmful ways, just like he "knew" about my two friends early in our marriage. So if he tells me someone is not to be trusted, I need to figure out if his belief is emerging from that deep source of knowledge or from being heavily medicated. How do I honor his sense of things, respect his nearly foolproof compass, but also allow for the influence of mind-bending drugs?

"Babe," I venture gently, "remember how sometimes medication can do goofy things in our minds? The stuff you took to stop the spasms might be making you a little paranoid."

He listens and nods his head in understanding. But he is not comforted, nor is it reducing his fears. His eyes look a little wild. I'm desperate to bring peace to his mind when I remember our trauma therapy training. For each fear and negative belief, there is an alternate and opposing positive belief, even if the former seems ever so much stronger than the latter. Maybe we can find a positive belief to occupy his mind. I take a breath, hoping and praying—when am I not in that state anymore?—for some emotional salve for him and for me, too. I pose the question to Reuel.

"When those fears begin to grab you and try to convince you of things, what is it you would prefer to believe instead?"

He grows quiet and then closes his eyes. Is he experiencing another wave of pain or fear? Has my question even registered in any meaningful way? Suddenly he looks up with startlingly clear eyes and declares, "The Divine and I together have the strength to defeat anything."

Breathtaking! What clarity and concise truth from such a befuddled brain. It's a perfect antidote to fears, I realize as I watch him. Just saying the words aloud has made a difference in him. His face has relaxed, his body is calmer, and he emanates a sense of both peace and empowerment. He looks at me, and I can see Reuel is back, inhabiting his mind again.

"Thank you." He smiles with the faintest trace of a tear lurking.

"We are a team," I quickly reply, wanting to head off any sentiment that would bruise our overripe hearts. His spirit seems to settle, and I glance at the clock. Time for me to get home and get some sleep. I tuck him in. We repeat the positive and powerful belief together and kiss each other goodnight before I walk those long corridors alone once more.

The sleep is short-lived. I get a phone call before sunrise the next morning. My heart pounds with fear of calamity. It is Reuel, speaking so softly I can't understand him. I keep telling him I can't hear until he finally raises his voice enough.

"I'm trapped in the hospital," he whispers in despair. "The nurses won't let me call you. No, I haven't had much sleep. They are trying to control things, and the nurses have to go along with it."

"Who is trying to control things?" I ask in my groggy state, assuming he was thinking logically.

"I can't say. They might hear." My heart wrenches at the terror in his voice, and I am fully awake.

"Remember how we talked about the ways the medication can make you fearful?" I attempt to reach his good sense, not knowing if the drugs have totally hijacked his rational mind. But he suddenly is coherent.

"Fears are real, but they're not necessarily reality." Yes! Thank God he understands. "I know this, but please can you get right over here? I'm still scared, and I need you to help me make sense of it."

He has more confidence in my ability than I do. How do I make sense of any of this? What sense can be made of such a vital, larger-than-life person reduced to living in four-hour doses between measures of pain medication? What kind of logic is to be found from the fact that his body is resisting all forms of chemotherapy and the lymphoma is running crazy through his blood and bones? Stop. I can't go there. I can't hover on that thought and still care for Reuel, my clients, and myself. The next chemo cocktail HAS to be the one that works.

Thank God the hospital staff kept coffee going in the family room on the floor. I grab their biggest cup, fill it to the brim, and head to Reuel's room. He greets me with a pained expression, brow furrowed, looking down, occasionally glancing up at me with a pleading expression, like he knows something isn't quite right in his mind. I wonder again if I should have stayed the night with him, but Reuel himself, as well as some of the staff, have been insistent that I go home to get good rest for this medical marathon we're running.

I scoot my chair up to the bed, take his hand, and express how sorry I am that his night was so scary. His shoulders relax. He looks at me with watery eyes and brings my hand up to his heart.

"This is hard. I'm doing this for you, for us, and for our kids, our family. I want to grow old with you, and I want to know all my grandkids." There is no paranoia here. This is the most lucid statement he's made in quite some time.

"I know how much we mean to you," I replied, my own eyes gathering tears. "I can't imagine what strength and courage you've had to draw on. I am so grateful you're willing to do this for us, yet it seems an unfair request to make of you."

He is quiet now, whether from the intimacy of the moment, the pain, or the exhaustion of the nightmares. He drifts off to sleep. Every once in a while he opens an eye, checks on my presence, then returns to sleep.

I pick up the notebook Marci and I share, and I see an entry in her handwriting that states, "Dad is in the middle of molecular reorganization and restructuring right now."

"WHAT?" my brain shrieks. "What does that mean, and who said it?" Molecular reorganization? My mind races to understand. I take deep breaths. Some unwanted truth is tapping my shoulder.

Inside Look: Office, Late Career

The voice on the message sounds desperate. She gives her first name, Kate, and says her friend, another of my clients, referred her. "I just learned some devastating news," then I hear sobs and several beats of silence before she asks for an appointment. "It's an emergency. I don't know how I'm going to make it." I take down her number and feel my shoulders slump. This has all the markings of a wife who just learned her husband had an affair.

Unfortunately, I am correct. Kate is obviously attractive, I note as she sits in the corner chair the next day, even with the dark circles under her eyes and the drawn mouth. I also remind myself that attractiveness has very little to do with a partner's infidelity. She describes her story to me in fits and starts, sometimes appearing to be in shock, sometimes sobbing to breathlessness. Her husband of twenty-five years suddenly decided to be honest with her and confessed multiple occasions of infidelity over the years. He now wants to make a "fresh start" with her since the kids are grown and thought she'd be grateful he was coming clean. He has thrust the marriage to a crossroads.

The initial therapy with someone in her situation resembles therapy with a sudden trauma survivor, and indeed it is traumatic for the one betrayed. It's essential that she tell her story in her time and that she knows that I can listen and help contain not only her story but also all the emotions that surround it. There will be many issues to address in her healing process, but right now I have to raise a topic that usually adds to the betrayed's sense of shame and dread.

"Kate, before we close I need to raise something you may not have considered. Because of the prevalence of many types of sexually transmitted diseases, it is important for you to get tested."

"What? But I . . . But he . . . But I'm too embarrassed to go to my doctor. She knows my husband also!"

"There are good alternatives here in the community that provide testing services, and you don't even have to give your name. It's imperative for your health. If you do test positive, you can get treated right away. If your test results are negative, then it won't take up any more emotional or mental energy."

She hangs her head but nods in agreement. If any

fragments of denial remain in her mind, they have just been vaporized.

···

Crossroads come in all long-term relationships. They can provide an opportunity to slow down and gain bearings as you approach the upcoming intersection and even reconfirm your goals or destination. At other times, a couple may be suddenly thrust into a crossroads, narrowly avoiding a smash-up. Or a crash at a particular junction may be unescapable.

One of the biggest crossroads Reuel and I encountered was totally unanticipated. What we thought would be a pleasant afternoon drive in the marital countryside changed drastically in an instant. Suddenly we were careening into a dangerous relationship intersection, dodging speeding oncoming issues.

This particular crossroads journey began not long after our thirtieth anniversary party, when we decided to tour Napa Valley. Reuel had been taking intensive wine training courses and developing his palate into a sophisticated and accurate tasting apparatus, so what better place to let it loose than California wine country?

We were busy making preparations for the trip when my gynecologist's office called. The results from my annual pap exam indicated a repeat test was necessary. Okay, no problem; that occasionally happens. A week later, however, we were about to leave for the airport when the doctor herself called to say the results confirmed dysplasia due to HPV.

I had worked for doctors, had advanced training in sex therapy, and thought I was pretty savvy about medical diagnoses. But I'd never heard of HPV. Most people hadn't heard of it back then, let alone thought about a vaccine for it.

"What is that?" I asked the doctor.

She hesitated. "The kind you have is a sexually trans-mitted disease. It can be dormant in your body for years and then be triggered due to stress. For example, I had a patient who was a nun who had it. Even though she was celibate, she had been sexually abused as a child. It had stayed dormant within her until her sixties. At any rate, we'll need to treat this because it can be destructive in women."

"What about my husband?"

"Men carry it, but it doesn't do damage to them. It's you we need to treat." She went on to explain the upcoming proce-dure.

I hung up and put my head between my knees. *An STD? Me?* Never had I imagined those letters in any of my medical records. How did this happen? I flashed to Reuel's frustrations with our sex life. Had he had an affair? My mind raced backwards to review everything I knew about him.

No. I was sure he had not. We had had too many dis-cussions about the consequences of an affair in marriage, and he always told me about encounters with co-workers or choir members and the steps he'd taken to "affair-proof" our mar-riage. But, the other side of my brain argued that maybe all the pain he had had and the sessions of EMDR were to treat his guilt from an affair.

No. As I raised my head I knew deep within me, throughout my whole system, that was not the case. He had not had an affair.

I took a deep breath and explained the phone conversation to a worried Reuel. He took my hand and looked directly into my eyes. "I want you to know, even though you may not need me to say it, that I have never cheated on you and have never even wanted to have an affair. You're the one I'm still crazy about."

I couldn't speak for a while. It was exactly what I needed to hear, and he knew to say the words to me.

"The same is true for me," I eventually said, "but where could it have come from? Didn't you tell me about some sexual experimentation you did as a kid?"

"Yes, when I was about twelve, with a neighbor kid."

"Well then, that's where it came from," I resolved, tucking that scary issue back into the box. I stood up to finish packing.

"No!" Reuel stood fierce, immovable. "This is not something you will slide off on me. It's too easy to attribute it to something I did, without looking at yourself and your own history. I will not be a party to that. This is something you've got to figure out for yourself."

Stunned, I sat back down. This was a new Reuel. Not the man who always gave compassionately when I was in pain, but the man giving me back my own stuff to deal with instead of taking it on himself. That was different, and I didn't like it. I wasn't even sure what he was talking about. What did I need to figure out for myself?

All further conversation was tabled while we scrambled to make the flight to San Francisco and meet our friends for the drive to Sonoma County. They caught the strain and silences between Reuel and me, but I wasn't ready to explain it to them. I didn't fully understand it myself.

As the long weekend proceeded, I began to understand some things. Reuel was mad. Then I was mad. What right did he have to be angry? This was happening to my body, not his. Again! We were in an emotional flashback from twenty years before, when I was to undergo radiation for thyroid cancer. I thought we had already learned this lesson. I thought we had mastered this route. But no, we were detouring into a new crossroads. I was once again dodging Reuel's anger and trying to drive through the fog of my own confusion while also trying to find passage for our friends, with whom we'd planned this getaway.

It was probably a good thing that we had planned a trip to wine country instead of Amish country for that weekend. Tasting wine as an art is full of sensuous experiences: visual treats of golds and burgundies, bouquets of light honeysuckle or deep blueberries filling the nose, and bursts of flavor—grapefruit, butterscotch, blackberry, smoke, leather. The senses demand immediacy. Standing at the winery's counter, swirling and sipping, comparing notes, we were totally present. It was the perfect antidote to the emotions flinging us from dreadful past into dreaded future. Especially since we weren't driving, becoming slightly tipsy didn't hurt either.

However, wine tasting didn't fill every hour of our days and nights. We talked about the diagnosis only a few times during the trip. I felt caught between what our friends wanted and what Reuel needed. The level of his angst and withdrawal didn't make sense to me if he was concerned about my health. The doctor had explained this was easily treatable at this stage and was not yet cancerous. I kept trying to engage him, thinking if he talked more about it, he could get over it and we could have more fun. He didn't cooperate. And hey, shouldn't this diagnosis bomb be about me, not him? Finally, our last day there, he suggested renting a car on our own to drive into the Russian River Valley. Later, we would meet our friends for dinner. *Fine*, I thought, *maybe this will pull him out of his funk.*

We drove north on back roads through autumn-drenched vineyards. The rolling grape fields captivated us with their purple clusters crowding the vines. We noted which wineries to revisit in the future, talked to a winemaker about that year's harvest, and soon enough the setting sun let us know we needed to head back for our dinner meetup.

Not long into the drive back, Reuel announced, "I am not going to dinner with them tonight."

"But," I stammered, appalled. "They love last-night-of-trip celebration dinners. I think they'll be hurt."

"That's unfortunate, but I really don't want to do it tonight."

I was caught between wanting to celebrate with our friends and my husband, whose mood would be even blacker if I chose them over him. He glanced at me and frowned.

"I just told you what I want. We know what the friends want. What is it *you* want?"

I had no idea what I wanted. I knew what I didn't want—for our friends to be hurt, for Reuel to be hurt, especially for him to be mad. My insides felt like the vat of pressed grapes we had just seen at the last winery.

He repeated the question.

"Well, I know it means a lot to Rob and Sarah to meet them."

"No!" he interrupted. "Not what they want. What do

you want?"

I was silent for some time. "I don't want you to be so moody." Wrong answer. He looked even more thunderous. "I don't know what I want!" I blurted. "I feel so caught in the middle, it hurts. I don't know what to do!"

"You do seem very caught in the middle," he softened. "Why do you need to take care of their feelings or mine?"

Ha! If I didn't take care of his feelings, he'd be even more angry and brooding. Somewhere in my brain flashed a bolt of recognition that I was managing him. Drat! I'm not supposed to be doing that, either.

"Would you just check inside," Reuel said, "and see what it is you really want for yourself this evening?"

What I wanted was to minimize the fallout of my decision. I had been crying and felt wrung out, so I knew I wasn't going to offer scintillating conversation that night. Meeting our friends felt more stressful at that point, so I told Reuel I'd like to have dinner with him.

He tilted his head at me and nodded. We drove in silence in the waning daylight. I didn't feel like eating, but we had the evening to get through. After a few miles, Reuel spoke again.

"I believe there's a connection between you not knowing what you want and how you reacted to the HPV diagnosis."

Well duh, I thought, *since the diagnosis blindsided me and turned what I knew upside down*. I might have said that out loud, or else Reuel could tell from my expression what I was thinking, because he continued with more determination.

"You are one of the strongest people I know, and together we have accomplished some amazing things. We have each done good work on ourselves, but now we are at a cross-roads."

My stomach flipped. Where was he going with this?

"One of the patterns that got set up through the years, a pattern we co-constructed, was that if things got too uncomfortable or intense for you, I would relieve you of some of that intensity by taking it on myself. Sometimes that meant picking up extra responsibility around the house, which was okay. But sometimes it meant accepting responsibility for what was really yours. I guess I didn't trust you could fully handle it yourself, and that wasn't fair to you."

I was too exhausted to be defensive, so I let him continue.

"When you tried to put the blame for HPV on me and my childhood history, it hit me like a ton of bricks what our pattern had been. I could have taken the blame, felt ashamed about how once again we believed my family was worse than yours. You would have reassured me, and we would have gone on.

"The problem is that when we act like it's all me or my family, you don't go deeper to examine you and your family. What might be you and your family gets sealed in a compartment. And here's the thing . . ." I held my breath. "When you don't examine yourself, it keeps you from knowing yourself."

"But I thought that's exactly what I've been doing all this time, especially since the thyroid cancer."

"You have been, yes." He hesitated. "What I'm saying now is that I am no longer going to prevent you from facing those sealed compartments. You have to look at those if we're going to have the marriage we want."

I was silent. Reuel looked at me every once in a while, offering nonverbal reassurance, but he knew to let me be. At this crossroad, I faced the prospect of uncovering and opening a new Pandora's Box. Not for the first time, I wondered if the courage demanded to make this journey was worth it.

22
Healing

Second Week of March

Reuel has been hospitalized for about four weeks now and has been clearheaded for a week. It is beyond joyful to have him back, or at least to have his mind back with us. I feel more hopeful and less lonely, even though he still struggles with fears. Well, who wouldn't be afraid, I think to myself, *but at least these more recent fears are not the para-noid, Mafioso type brought on by the narcotics.*

Marci finishes work early and joins us in her dad's hospital room. The three of us visit. Reuel, now that he is no longer confused, catches up with Marci's life. In the silent spaces, though, I can see Reuel's fears working on him. Suddenly I have an idea. I weigh the uncertainty of proceeding in Marci's presence, but it seems surpris-ingly right. So I ask Reuel if he wants to use EMDR to help allay his fears. He does.

One of the first things we must do in this technique is target a specific disturbing scene, then identify the negative thoughts associat-ed with it. Reuel blurts out his negative thinking even before targeting a scene: "If I'm by myself, something bad happens. I'm destined to do something wrong." *I write it quickly on my notepad, because the neg-ative beliefs often are difficult to wrangle, and I don't want to miss it.*

No sooner do I finish writing than Reuel identifies the scene that accompanies his belief. "I see myself in Barbados, but I am all alone. I am by myself all the time." Marci and I glance at each other. Reuel catches us, and says, "I know, it surprises me too."

He follows my fingers back and forth as I lead him through the first round of EMDR. What emerges, while heartbreaking to hear, isn't as much a surprise to me as to our daughter. She quietly listens, takes some notes, and sheds a few tears as she hears her father process some of the deepest experiences that formed him.

"It was inevitable that I would die, and it would somehow be my own fault," he explains, "because I deserved to die. How I died was immaterial, nor would I take anyone with me in my death since I am the only one responsible." I am writing madly to capture the essence of his processing.

He continues. "If I did anything wrong, I deserved to die, and it was not possible to do it right, so my death was inevitable. Talking about it would have been to indulge in pity, so I just needed to accept the inevitable." He takes a few shallow breaths.

I ask him where that belief is located in his body. Uncharacteristically, he refuses to answer. We wait. Finally he replies, "If I locate it in my body, it will condemn me all the more."

But then his brain begins to connect some dots in a different way. "Oh, if I locate the belief, it can change. It can be an agent of change, not an agent of weakness." He moves his hands to his lower chest to locate the belief and accompanying fear, and describes it as dark yellow in color. I am reminded of the same imagery he used with Sharon several weeks before when he was still home.

"An incredible strength is needed to fight the inevitability of dying," he states. "Do I possess that? Am I aware enough?"

Oh, *I think*, if you are not strong enough or not aware enough, then there's little hope for the rest of us.

"I have a sense of the Divine," he comments, "and the Divine is letting me know 'I want you there, but you have to decide.'" That triggers disbelief in Reuel. "It doesn't seem possible; it feels like a cheap trick."

I'm not sure what is happening, or where it is the Divine wants him, but I keep quiet.

At this point, Marci puts her hands on his chest, about where he thought the fear was located, and asks him if he could feel her hands.

"Yes, but the touch is confusing. This message is too difficult, and I shouldn't have involved you. I'm afraid I've just worried you. I don't want you to have the worry. That worry helped me survive as a kid, and I've thought our family's survival depended on my worry, too."

He's getting very choked up, can hardly get the words out, but is driven to ask her, "Have I damaged you? Hurt you? Have I burdened you beyond your ability? I'm afraid I have not been enough."

"No!" Marci cries. "Dad, you have been enough. You have been an amazing father." He looks in wonder at her, checking her sincerity and spirit. He glances at me, awash in my own tears, as if needing to confirm she is speaking from her heart. I nod.

It is palpable, the way we're allowing these truths to penetrate us as tears continue, cleansing and bonding us. After several moments Reuel speaks again, this time in a stronger voice.

"It's odd, the tone and tenor of how my body feels. My voice sounds different to me, from front to back. I have some love in my body that wasn't there before. I can feel it right here." He gestures over his heart. Then he looks up with strength and surprise. "My need to not make any mistakes is gone. The need to beat death is not such an all-powerful thing. It's such a relief!"

I don't know why, but I reach out and rub his chest. Maybe I want to touch the new love, or seal it in so it can't escape. He smiles. "This new love, the un-burdensome love, is pale yellow, and it used to be harsh yellow. It's now soft and warm." Marci and I are envisioning that soft yellow glow when Reuel abruptly turns toward her with concern in his eyes. "I want you to have the freedom to answer honestly about being burdened."

She repeats her affirmation of him as a father. "And this time I want you to hear it with your new heart." She reaches out and places her hand on his heart, noting how calm it feels to her, cool under her palm and warm out by her fingertips. He looks at her, closes his eyes, smiles, then looks at her again. We absorb that for a while.

Next, I encourage Reuel to identify a positive belief he can hang onto, especially if the negative message starts to creep back. It doesn't take him long before he declares, "The strength of my relationship with the Divine is unbreakable." I write it on the chalkboard where he can see it from his bed, and then we begin saying good night.

Marci and I walk out to the parking lot together, exhausted but peaceful, still in awe at what had occurred during the evening.

I don't tell Marci, but tucked away in a niche within me is the thought this might be the turning point in his illness, the place from which the lymphoma begins receding and he is healed. Certainly he received an emotional healing tonight, so why wouldn't the physical healing follow? Maybe he won't even have to do another round of chemotherapy because there will be such remarkable changes in his upcoming blood tests.

Inside Look: MFT Classroom, Early Mid-Career

"Class, I've just finished training in a new trauma

technique, and it's blowing my mind. It's called EMDR, which stands for Eye Movement Desensitization & Reprocessing." Students were listening, but faces were blank.

"This is going to sound a little woo-woo, but they're starting to develop quite a research base to support the effectiveness of this approach." I paused to figure out how to best explain this.

"Why do you say it's 'woo-woo'?" One student couldn't wait.

"Well, the gist of it is that by moving your eyes back and forth rapidly, it accesses the part of your brain that can help to process the trauma." *Oh dear, they look more confused than ever.* "Okay, you'll remember that when there's trauma, our brains get so overwhelmed, they don't know where to file the incoming data—information which is too much, too fast, and too awful. As a result, the trauma data just sit there, not just in our brains but also our bodies, waiting to get resolved. That's often what flashbacks are about—the trauma data reappearing, trying to figure out where to get filed in our brains, so the data can finally be settled."

"And the eye movements file the trauma information?" One student's question was reflected on the faces of most of the class. I understood the confusion.

"Well, the eye movements don't file the trauma, but they access the deep processing that didn't yet happen. The beautiful thing is that the client's brain knows exactly what to do with that data and where to file it because our bodies, including our brains, move towards healing. You know that if we have infection in a wound, it has to get cleared out before the wound can fully heal. Same with trauma. It has to get cleared out or filed away before it can fully heal. Even if two people shared the same traumatic experience, their brains store the incoming traumatic data differently. Healing, then, depends on each one's brain being able to access the fragments of memories and organize them in ways that are meaningful and healing for that person.

"We as therapists can help provide a framework for the clearing out (which is what the training is all about), but we also need to stay out of the way of the client's organic process. Your brain knows best how to heal you, just as my brain knows best how to heal me, and their brain knows best how to heal them."

....

After our emotionally loaded Napa "vacation," figuring Reuel maybe had a point about needing to know myself better, I decided to go back into therapy. I wanted to solve the mystery about my avoidance and compartmentalization. And what the hell did it mean that I had HPV? My work with clients was as solid as ever, but outside the office I felt a bit tenuous, as if the mortar between the bricks of my selfhood had softened to a squishy consistency.

My therapist tried to help, but my unconscious had such tightly guarded defenses it wasn't about to reveal who was responsible for the HPV. That was locked up beyond the reach of talk therapy. I needed a different approach—EMDR— so I got a referral and set an appointment.

Unknown to me at the time, during one of his meditation moments, Reuel had become certain that I had been sexually abused by a relative. He even "saw" two details about the person—he had a tattoo and had done military service. He felt it was important not to share this information until I discovered it for myself. He could then confirm my new awareness. Reuel told me later he wondered how long he would have to keep it to himself—months? years? —because my defenses were so strong.

As it turned out, he didn't have to hold the information very long. One night, as we were getting ready for bed, I got extremely antsy. I couldn't sit down, I couldn't stand still, and I couldn't stand being in my own skin. I began to talk to Reuel, which usually relaxed me, but I got even more restless. My body was buzzing with anxiety, my mind racing, my heart pounding, my emotional equilibrium tipping.

Reuel, meanwhile, sensed that my uneasiness was about the source of the STD, which he cautiously mentioned to me. I agreed and felt even more anxious, like I might levitate right off the bed.

My head was spinning, packed to the brim with thoughts. I tried to grasp specifics out of the spin cycle. Sexual . . . family . . . abuse . . . man . . . not father . . . Uncle Paul? Grandpa? No! It couldn't be grandpa, who taught me to make flapjacks on the outdoor griddle, let me run in the pasture, and allowed me to be as messy as I wanted. A new swirl of thoughts erupted. I finally voiced some of them to Reuel.

"Yes," he said. "I understand. I was given information for you for this point in your recognition."

Whoa. "What?! What were you given?"

He told me about the tattoo and military service.

"But that could be either Uncle Paul or my grandpa." I wailed, afraid I wouldn't get any more clarity.

"Whose name or face came to you first?"

"Uncle Paul."

"Then that's your truth," Reuel said. "I know what your grandpa meant to you, but I think his image came up to confuse you and keep you from the truth."

My body calmed, the spinning thoughts slowed, and understanding was a balm. It was an "a-ha" throughout my whole system—body, mind, and spirit—and the truth of it permeated all my cells.

As I began to make sense of it aloud, I described Uncle Paul's tattoo on his arm, his career in the Navy. I wondered when the abuse could have happened, because he visited infrequently. The most likely time was when we lived in California, while dad was in Mortuary College and Uncle Paul was stationed nearby.

"But that means I would have been three or four years old." The awfulness of it swept over me and over Reuel. We leaned against the headboard, emotionally drained. I gripped Reuel's hand, breaking contact only when I reached for a tissue or shuddered with the realization. Even so, relief prevailed and returned after each shudder and sob. The knowledge provided a healing and another intimate connection with Reuel.

Despite the peace that came from finally knowing the truth, the truth alone was not enough to fully heal the traumatic experience. For that, I needed to do some EMDR.

For me, the trauma processing did not involve cognitive memories of the incident of abuse—not surprising because

I was so young when it happened. However, my body had stored emotional memories. During the trauma therapy, waves and waves of terror washed over me. Sometimes, I was too frightened to cry, until gradually the waves of fear calmed to peace. Other times, I felt such tension I thought my muscles might snap. Moments later, I would feel prickling, numbing, tingling, and tickling. The EMDR sessions were unpredictable and exhausting. Always, though, the sensations subsided, and I felt increasingly unburdened and clear.

After a few appointments, when most of the early abuse had been cleared, I began to notice occasional nagging abdominal cramps. After a few weeks, they became more frequent and more draining. I researched the symptoms of lactose intolerance and decided that fit with what I was feeling. The results of my diet adjustments were inconsistent, and I still spent too much time huddled up with cramps.

"Don't you have an EMDR session coming up soon?" Reuel asked one morning as we got ready for work.

"Tomorrow, before I go to the office."

"I think you should work on the lactose intolerance with EMDR." He threw out the suggestion off-handedly.

Weird, I thought, but Reuel had been on target with too many things for me to dismiss his idea. I thought about his suggestion as I drove home that night. Lactose intolerance . . . milk . . . mother's milk . . . Damn! This is about my mother. Now I knew I had to address it with EMDR.

The therapist was a bit surprised when I told her the target for processing the next day, but as usual, she set up the light box with the horizontally sliding light she used in EMDR. I focused on the cramping, held the associated negative belief in mind—something like "I'm doomed"—and followed the light back and forth with my eyes. This gave my brain free reign to take me where it needed to go.

"Lactose . . . intolerance . . . lactose . . . intolerance" my mind sing-songed—"lactose" at the far left light, "intolerance" at the far right. Images from childhood flashed like a slide show through my mind. Then the word lactose disappeared, changing to "intolerance . . . intolerance . . . in . . . tolerance . . . In . . . tolerance."

Oh! The realization hit like a ton of bricks and blasted through my defensive shield. I lived in too much tolerance! The problem with my family was one of too much tolerance—of things that were toxic—and not enough tolerance of growing young minds and spirits.

I had already worked through the toxic exposure to my father, but this slant on my mother was new. The EMDR process continued to unfold further understandings: My mother had had too much tolerance for things that should not have been tolerated. My brother and I suffered because of her tolerance of my father's behavior. My mother didn't have enough boundaries, and I was at risk of not having enough boundaries if I focused more on what others needed without attending to what I needed. The abdominal cramping was trying to let me know about boundaries. Incredible! This lactose intolerance was about the danger of living in too much tolerance and without adequate boundaries!

I left the session both dazed and solidified. During the next week, I had almost no appetite. The cramps were gone, but the only food I could stomach was mixed nuts. How symbolic of my family! I laughed about that as I described it to my office colleague.

"Oh," she explained, "your body is reorganizing after that major shift you had with EMDR."

Huh. Emotional healing indeed led to physical healing.

Some days later, Reuel woke at 3 a.m. with an image of me cloaked by a grey veil of positive, strong, healing energy. He heard in his heart, "She is a fearsome warrior in the struggle she is going through, and the battle is almost complete. She is being healed."

When Reuel described to me what happened next, I asked him to write it up so we would have a record of it. He wrote:

> The energy around the image and the message was one of warmth, strength, quiet confidence, very positive, enveloped in healing. Immediately following that image and message, I was given the sense that Judy has come through the worst of her pain and is being healed. No timeline was given as to when the battle would be complete.
>
> I returned to bed and began praying for Judy's healing. Having witnessed the pain she has gone through, I asked the Divine to heal her as soon as possible. As part of that prayer, I asked to be given a role in bringing healing to Judy. I then reached over and with three fingers — to represent the Father, Son, and Spirit — lightly touched the top layer of the blanket covering her. I did not want to wake her, just wanted to touch the hem of her blanket.
>
> At this point Judy, the notoriously heavy sleeper, awoke. She saw me leaning over her and asked if she'd been snoring and had woken me.
>
> "No, you weren't snoring," I said.

"Why did you nudge me?" she asked.

"I hardly touched you, in fact just barely touched the blanket," I told her.

She said, "Oh, well, I was having a horrible nightmare, and I felt your touch. It took me out of the nightmare."

Years passed, and I forgot about that incident until after Reuel died. I was going through bottomless piles of papers, and there was his note about the nightmare and healing. I doubled over in grief when I read it. I'd always known his role in my healing was huge, ever since the early days of our relationship. What took my breath away this time was his intentional use of three fingers. He had used our personal code—three fingers—to express a love beyond the two of us on a spiritual plane that furthered my healing. One finger at a time: I . . . Love . . . You.

23
"It's Enough"

"I define connection as the energy that exists between people
when they feel seen, heard, and valued; when they can give and
receive without judgment; and when they derive sustenance and
strength from the relationship."
—Brené Brown

Second to Third Week of March

*I feel unexpectedly hopeful after Reuel's experience of healing from
harsh yellow to soft yellow. I think about how color embodied energy
within him and wonder how my fundamentalist-groomed skepticism
of auras and chakras has limited my openness to Spirit. I glance at
Reuel, whose own spirit continues to be profoundly peaceful, and I
can't deny that energy seems to be shifting within him. In my mind, I
can almost hear the hum of healing happening.*

*Which is why the blood chemistry results delivered by the
doctor twenty minutes later are devastating. The lymphoma had
spread to 60% of his bone marrow. I am stunned. Reuel appears less
shaken. Does the doctor standing in the doorway deliberately not enter our room fully? Does bad news create the need for the oncologist's
quick exit? He informs us that the next round of chemo is put on the
fast track, and then he disappears.*

Okay, I think to myself, it's another hurdle to jump, and THEN we'll be on the road to recovery. Maybe the healing hasn't had time to show up in the blood work. I remember that message from almost nine months ago that Reuel would be okay. Doesn't that mean the same thing it meant when I had cancer? Slow down. The thing before us right now is another and different kind of chemo. This one, then, is—must be—the lymphoma solution.

We wait for the newest toxins to be ordered up from the pharmacy. My mood, like the hospital room, grows grayer and more dismal. If Reuel is going to be here for another week of chemo, then we need to jazz it up. I put out an electronic call for ideas. Coworkers bring him his photos of Italy from his work cubicle. Dear friends from Nigeria bring beautiful fabric panels that splash the walls with colors of the sun. Reuel doesn't feel up to seeing these friends, but at least the room looks brighter. Maybe that will help our spirits.

Social workers on the unit talk to us about where we want Reuel to be transferred for rehabilitation. I stare at them blankly. They explain that since Reuel has lost so much strength and may still need on-call medical aid, when it's finally time to discharge him, they will not discharge him to home. Oh. I am confused why they are asking about this now when he's due for more chemotherapy.

"Does that mean a nursing home?" I ask. "Or a section of the hospital?" And do most people have a rehab center on their list of preferred things, like hair stylists or chiropractors?

The polite social worker explains that rehab centers can be in hospitals, nursing homes, or specific facilities, then gives us two or three referrals to check.

The next day, Marci and I head out to get a feel for where Reuel might be transferred.

The first one we check has a cramped parking area in the back of an overweight building barely contained by its lot. It is hemmed in by a busy street at the front and massive snow piles on each side. Marci looks at the dark back entrance, then at me.

"This is not for my dad!" she cries in horror. "I can already smell it and we aren't even out of the car."

I put the car in reverse and we drive to the next place. It looks so uninviting that we don't even stop. We finally find one place with beautiful floor tile highlighting the décor. There are no smells; Reuel's sensitive nose would not be in danger here.

Heading back to the hospital, we decide to pick up some Boston Market to eat with Reuel. Marci and I are so engrossed in talking about finding a nursing facility that I almost miss the sudden brake lights of the car ahead. I slam on the brakes to avoid a rear-end collision. Great orange globs of hot macaroni and cheese fly through the car, landing on the dashboard, oozing down Marci's winter coat and my new leather purse. We are aghast at the close call and the sloppy mess around us. Then we erupt in laughter. By the time I pull into the hospital parking lot, we are still cackling and snorting so hard I can barely park the car. We run into the nearest restroom to wipe off the mac and cheese, giggling when we catch each other's eyes in the mirror. Strange how the ordeal is so renewing.

The next few days are filled with my clients, hospital visits, updating friends and family, and practicing the mindfulness of prayer. Our oldest—between contracts from his job as a pastry chef on a cruise ship—returns from visiting his brother in New York City. I ask him to make a big cake to thank the nursing unit personnel, a task he eagerly accepts. He edges the sheet cake with swirls of butter cream buds and writes our gratitude to the nurses in cursive chocolate across the top. He delivers it to the nursing station early Monday morning, and the cake is promptly devoured. Reuel could win "most popular patient" today for all the happy traffic popping in to thank him.

The next day, Tuesday, the oncologist spots me in the hall and pulls me aside.

"We are exhausting the possibilities, and the risk of infection has increased dramatically. We can't transfer Reuel to rehab because that risk is so high." He looks at me. His eyes say he wants me to understand something. The nurse calls him away.

Time takes on a suspended quality. I walk down the hall for more coffee and see the doctor working on charts.

I stop in front of him, wait until he makes eye contact, and ask the dreaded question: "Is there any hope left?"

"We can always hope," he replies. It is a distinctly unsatisfying response. I probably sounded like yet one more desperate family member. How many dozens of times has he responded with that platitude?

I return to Reuel's room, fresh coffee in hand. His eyes are bright and he is eager to talk. We have three hours before I have to go to the office, so I pull up a chair. We pretend we're home on the deck, reviewing our week. As in the last two weeks, he is totally present — the essence of Reuel — engaged, playful, wanting to know more. He has no memory of the first three weeks when the narcotics played with his mind.

I describe to him snippets of that time: the funny things he said, how he wanted to hook up the IV tube for a direct pipeline to ice cream, his horrified expression when he first saw the catheter tube and how hard I worked to suppress my laugh at his reaction. He shakes his head as we laugh together, and I can see him wondering how so much could have happened without his awareness. Then I describe how horrifying it was to accompany him to the scan to rule out metastasis to the brain.

"That was a bad day," I say, catching a sob in my throat.

His eyes fill with tears, and he takes my hand. "I'm so sorry you had to go through that."

I update him on the kids but have to rely on Aaron's reports from Cory, our youngest in New York, since we haven't received any direct calls from him. Reuel tries to reassure me.

"It's not that Cory doesn't care," he says, "but he doesn't know how to handle the intensity of his caring and his feelings. So he tries to block it out. He avoids. And eventually his body gets his attention. He's not unlike his father."

He looks at me with a twinkle, and we both remember the antique antacid tablet in his dresser drawer. He kept it as a souvenir from a previous girlfriend almost forty years ago to remind him not to take his feelings out through his stomach.

This really is like a conversation around our kitchen table, I think. Reuel is not in much pain, and the nursing staff are leaving us alone. I tell him about friends who have been encouraging us and contacts I've made through the Caring Bridge website. Time both stands still and moves too fast. Reluctantly, I have to leave.

As I drive to the office, I plead, laying out a case to the Divine for how much Reuel is loved and how wonderful it would be if the Divine could just heal him so we could move on from this chapter. His clients, children, and friends need him, and certainly I need him. So it just makes so much sense that he would be healed.

Faintly, I see the audacity of me trying to convince the Divine what "made sense," and a bubble of laughter erupts as I wait at a stop light. Then through the moonroof, I catch a flutter of movement. An eagle is circling.

Ahhh. As Reuel would say, the Divine is generous.

That night after work is our American Idol *night. I pick up a bag of popcorn and make my way to his room. Marci and Aaron are already here talking to Reuel, who still has the same level of alertness as this morning. What relief! I give him an awkward hug and kiss — you'd think we would have learned how to work around the IV tubes by now.*

We pull our chairs around the bed. We crane our necks to get a good view of the wall-mounted television, critique the singers, and chat during the commercials. It strikes me how perfectly peaceful it is to be together right now, right here. This is what my grandma meant when she said, "It's enough just to be together."

I bask in the richness of it, catching Reuel's eyes once in a while. We share a meaningful smile. He is feeling it also. I begin to let down from the day, realizing how beat I am. I have some niggling concern I might be getting sick. Finally I stand and reluctantly tell them I need to go home and get to bed. Reuel quickly agrees, expressing the importance of me taking care of myself. I really don't want to go but slowly make my way to the door, hugs and kisses blown to each other in case I am sick.

"Babe," Reuel reminds me, "you always feel this way when you're really tired."

"You're right, but I just want to soak in every molecule and minute of this time together."

"Don't try to come in the morning. It's okay. Use the extra time to sleep," he says.

✉

As a child, I didn't really understand what my grandma meant when she first said that it was enough just to be together. Gradually, she taught me the meaning of being totally present to one another, having no agenda, attuning to each other. It was enough when she was present because I felt loved and at peace with her and with myself.

The best marriages know how to recognize or create these "it's enough to be together" times. Whatever irritations, differences, or conflicts a couple may struggle with, they also have segments of time when it is enough just to be together, to love and feel loved, to be at peace with one another. Those quality times are substantial counterbalances to the cumulative weight of daily hassles. All couples need them. They are momentary but crucial bridges over life's troubled waters.

A few months before Reuel was diagnosed with lymphoma, while we were blissfully unaware of the subversives in his body, he and his best friend, Doug, the stained-glass artist, took us (me and Gerilyn) on a Caribbean cruise. For all of the amazing events we packed into those seven days, what Doug remembers most is the morning coffee ritual. He arranged every night for a pot of coffee to be delivered at 5:45 a.m. He took it out on the veranda and waited until he heard stirrings from Reuel next door. Then he'd pour a cup and hand it across the divider to Reuel. The two of them would chat or watch for flying fish or enjoy the ocean in silence. "It's the little things," Doug said. It was sufficient for the two of them to share coffee and be together, totally in the present—an "it's enough" experience between friends.

Some of those "enough" moments have since become vivid snapshots in my mind: Reuel watching football while he rubs my feet; Reuel craning his neck to watch every possible jet coming in for a landing; Reuel catching my eye across the room at a party, his eyebrows waggling.

One event plays through my mind more like a video

than a snapshot, although I don't know exactly why. Maybe because it was such a profound comprehension of what it means to be in the present. Even now as I recall it, it plays out in my memory as present tense.

Finally! Friday is here with all its promise of relaxation and pleasure. The weather is perfect—one of those rare Minnesota spring days when I can feel the sun healing as it warms, with just enough humidity to relax my muscles. I finish work early, swing by the bank to deposit this week's client woes, and head home for some serious deck time. As the garage door rises, I see Reuel's car already tucked into its spot. He must have gotten off early too, so I excitedly dump my bags at the back door to see what he's up to. He's way ahead of me, already on the deck, about to open a bottle of wine. We hug and celebrate, basking in the late spring sun, watching whatever wildlife will appear in the wetlands behind the house.

Reuel shows me the bottle of wine he brought from the basement. "It's the latest Isenhower Wine Club shipment," referring to one of our favorite winemakers from Walla Walla, whose wine club, Friends of Isenhower, ships twice a year. Reuel is fairly humming with anticipation.

I run upstairs to change and when I return, Reuel has two glasses and the opened bottle on the patio table. He ceremoniously fills each glass to that imaginary one-third level as we watch the sunlight sparkle off the deep burgundy color. We swirl, we sniff, then we toast to this diamond of an afternoon, and I experience my first Cabernet Franc.

Suddenly I'm transported back to my hometown of Walla Walla, to the county fair on Labor Day weekend. I'm flooded with memories of playing clarinet in the outdoor band concert, wandering the barns and exhibits, and shelling peanuts in the grandstands as we watched the rodeo each night.

I become aware of Reuel watching me. "Reuel," I can barely get the words out, "this wine tastes and smells like Walla Walla!"

He grins at my wonder. "Isn't life great? Isn't wine wonderful? Does it get any better than this?"

We watch egrets and great blue herons fishing in the pond, snatching more frogs than fish. The geese family with their new goslings forms a flotilla at the other end of the pond. Reuel spots a muskrat gliding along, making slippery tracks. We sip our wine, enjoy the nature show, and catch up with each other. It is an afternoon of slowing down and releasing the bubbles of dreams as we share our hopes and visions and drives.

The afternoon saunters along, the wine glasses somehow refill themselves, and eventually I ask about the alcohol percentage in the wine. Reuel examines the label, blinks a few times, and looks at me with a surprised smile.

"Well," he explains, "there are usually some degrees of freedom in how they measure the alcohol, and this one's right up there near the maximum limit. That means it may even be one percent higher than what the label says." We both blink at that. We are feeling ourselves to be at some kind of maximum limit, so I stand up to get cheese and crackers.

Just then Reuel makes a declaration. "I guess we truly are Friends of Isenhower," he says, as we burst into slightly tipsy laughter.

There the memory video ends. What remains through-out the cells in my body is the deep understanding that we were fully present to our surroundings, our senses, and each other. We had accepted the embedded invitations to intimacy on our deck that day. It was enough just to be together.

24
Transformation

"Love protects us from nothing, even as it unexplainably
sustains us in all things."
—James Finley

March 21st

By morning I am refreshed. I start with clients at 8 a.m. Marci stops
by Reuel's room at 10 a.m. and leaves me a message that he is doing
fine. At noon, I call him to check in. The nurse answers his phone.

"You need to get over here," she tells me. "He's not doing
well."

I cancel my clients, including the one who's already in my
waiting room, and dash out the door. I call two friends on my way to
the hospital to inform them. They both offer to come.

"No, I think it's just another thing to get through," I say.
They make me promise to call as soon as I know more.

Heart pounding, I arrive at Reuel's room. Several people are
attending to him. I learn that the thrush in his throat has gotten so
bad he can't swallow. And he is bleeding from his rectum—they are
afraid he is hemorrhaging internally. For the moment, the bleeding
appears stopped, but they want to send him to intensive care.

"Does he have a directive?" the charge nurse asks.

"What?"

"Do you know what his intentions are for resuscitation?"

Oh, yes. *"Should I be calling in family?"*

"You may want to put them on alert," the doctor says.

I leave messages for Aaron and Marci to get here immediately and one for Cory in New York. I call my two friends back and update them. The local one tells me she's on her way. I am relieved I don't have to make the decision about whether she should come.

I go to Reuel as we wait for his transfer to ICU. His eyes seem so far away. They scare me. I get as close to him as the personnel and equipment allow. I hold his arm and smile, trying to reach him. His eyes flicker acknowledgement, but he is somewhere I can't reach. I am frightened in a new way.

Aaron arrives, and we hug tightly. We walk beside Reuel's gurney for the trek to ICU and then have to wait outside until they get him set in the new room. Mary, who has been a devoted friend since we started our Ph.D. programs together, arrives, followed by Marci. We all cling to each other. One of us is continually trying to reach Cory, whose phone sends every call to his voicemail.

We are allowed in with Reuel. We meet his ICU nurse, who will be constantly with him. His eyes are more focused, and he seems glad we are all here. His nurse knows the importance of our being together but doesn't let us stay with him for long.

There is a big, boisterous family in the ICU waiting area, celebrating their patriarch's successful passage through heart surgery. I can't stand to be around them . . . can't stand them. We find a different room, small, with hard-backed chairs facing each other so that our knees touch, but at least it is private.

"What about calling some of your friends?" Mary asks.

"Yeah, I guess." I know what's happening is serious, but it isn't conceivable that Reuel will not come out of it.

About 5:00 p.m., the nurse calls us back. She tells us she isn't getting his vital signs back to where they need to be. She wants to intubate him so his lungs don't have to work as hard. Okay.

"But, we have to put him out to do that, so you need to say your good-byes to him. We don't know if he will regain consciousness."

What? Oh, but you don't know Reuel, I think. Later, I would understand how merciful shock is to dull reality's razor.

Fine, we'll say goodbye, but this is not final, I insist to myself.

The kids gather around Reuel and say their goodbyes. I can't hear the specifics. Then they back away and turn to look at me.

I move in, sit on his bed, and lean over his face so he can hear me through the oxygen mask and see my eyes.

"I love you. I have been the most fortunate woman in the world to have you in my life. We have had the most incredible marriage." Tears are streaming down my face, and he reaches his hand to me. "I want to have more years with you in this marriage. But I trust you. And I trust the Divine."

He nods and flicks his eyes. How much does he know about what's happening? I say it again: "I love you. I trust you. I trust the Divine." I kiss his cheek and forehead, then step back to join the kids at his side.

The nurse enters, and we tell Reuel we'll see him in a little while. Suddenly, he starts waving his arms, gesturing to us. We look at him, check with each other, but none of us understands what he wants. Finally, he yanks off the oxygen mask, holds up his hand with his ring finger extended, and says to Marci, "The ring—"

Understanding washes over her face. "Yes, Dad, I know. It's okay, I've got it," she assures him. He nods, relaxes back into his pillow, puts the oxygen mask in place. We wave to him as we are led from the room.

On the way to our waiting area, my friend Lori from a town three hours away comes down the hall. Running to hug her, I ask, "What are you doing here?" incredulous she could have made it in such a short time.

"Well," she said, "I was in the middle of a session when I suddenly stood up, told the client I had to leave, and drove like hell to get here. I just knew I had to be here. Now where's Reuel?"

We update her, and she makes her way past the medical "guards" by declaring herself Reuel's sister. Meanwhile, we return to the waiting area, and I cancel more client appointments. Still no word from Cory. In a desperately inspired moment, I call the restaurant where he works, declare my emergency, and ask for the phone number of a coworker. The phone is answered, and yes, Cory is there. He croaks a hello and explains he has been throwing up for the last twenty-four hours. He is staying with his friend and forgot his phone in his apartment.

How do you tell your son, who has been out of contact for the last six weeks, that his dad is dying? I start, "Dad has taken a turn for the worse, and we want you to be here . . . " I say that his brother has been working on flights for him, but Cory is too weak to board a plane. I can tell he is dazed with this shocking news. He starts several sentences, most of them with "But . . ." There is no good way to answer the implied questions.

"It is a total shock," I confirm. "We keep thinking he's going to turn around with the next medical procedure, but he's not improving. His blood pressure keeps plunging. Cory, the nurse made us say

good-bye to him." Is Cory going to tip into shock himself?

"My dad is dying?" he keeps repeating, first as a weak question to himself, then growing to a bold sense of injustice.

We sign off, each of us to make plans for how to proceed. Lori returns from Reuel's side, somewhat pale. Each of us works a cell phone, contacting whoever needs to be called: clients, airlines, friends, extended family members.

Then it hits me: Oh dear God, how is Reuel's ninety-five-year-old mother going to survive this? I'll think about that later. Unbeknownst to me, Mary is calling my closest friends to gather for support. Lori is not on her phone, but looking around the room. Between calls, I notice her expression and ask if she is okay.

"Did you see that?" she asks hesitantly.

"See what?"

"I just saw Reuel. He came in to check on us. He's starting his Spirit journey."

My mind tries to grasp what she says, but there's only blankness. A journey? "But he's coming back, isn't he?" I can't take in the alternative.

She smiles gently at me. "He's incredibly peaceful and luminous."

That's good to hear. I want him to be peaceful. Then my mind starts protesting. It can't mean he's actually dying! Reuel had that assurance that he'd be okay. He can still pull out of this. Miracles happen. But we had to say goodbye. It can't mean . . . My mind is caught in a sickening loop.

We continue to peck away at our to-do lists. Lori disappears—I learn later she didn't want his body to be alone—and more friends assemble. The nurse specialist and the ICU specialist call me to his room, explaining that the measures they're taking are having no effect. They can hardly keep up with draining his lungs, they fill so quickly. His blood pressure continues to drop.

"Pretty soon it will reach a critical limit," they explain. "Do you want us to try to revive him?"

As opposed to what? I nod my head. The doctor assures me that's what he would do with a family member.

We take turns, then, one staying in the room and the others staying out of the way of the three or four professionals constantly attending to Reuel. My body shakes. I sit for a while. Then I have to leave to get different air. I meet another friend, newly arrived on the scene. Friends resuscitate my spirit with hugs and shared tears. A similar process is happening for Aaron and Marci with their friends. The kids and I return to Reuel's unit. We pray continually and witness heroic medical efforts until we need another breather.

Sometime before 9 p.m., the nurse turns to us where we are standing in the corner of the room.

"We're almost to that point. We don't know what he can hear, or what he knows, but it's time to say a final goodbye."

We get Cory on the phone, and one by one we stand beside Reuel, as close as we can get. I don't know if our goodbyes are spoken aloud or in our heads. We are so in sync with each other that I feel what each is saying.

Aaron moves the phone up to his dad's ear so Cory can say goodbye.

And we play out this last family time, Reuel's eyes closed and a cell phone to his ear, with a breathing apparatus, IVs, and other tubes in his body. Three of us are touching each other and Reuel's body, one of us connected via cell phone tower systems, all of us in varying stages of shock, all of us affirming the strength of our love and commitment to each other. I repeat my vow from my goodbye *when Reuel was conscious: "I trust you, and I trust the Divine." Reuel already knows that, but the truth of it empowers me, and I hope it empowers my kids or whoever is within earshot. Aaron brings the phone back to his own ear to check that Cory has said goodbye, then keeps him on the phone for whatever is next.*

The ICU specialist explains they have given Reuel enough medication to jump-start a race horse, but to no effect. His heart will soon flatline, and the doctor confirms with me the order to attempt resuscitation. Again I nod, and almost immediately Reuel's heart stops. A nurse asks if we want to stay in the room while they proceed with the attempt. We do, but I can't watch. I turn away from Reuel to face the wall. I hear the buzzing of the charger and the loud thump of his body as the electricity jolts him.

I hear this cycle four times before the doctor turns to me. "We can keep this up, but it will start to break bones and will have no effect. Should we stop?"

I look at my two kids—the products of the great life force that was Reuel and the outcome of such fierce and wonderful love—and they silently nod agreement. The staff ceases the struggle to retain life.

I thank them for their efforts, or at least I believe I have. The doctor holds out his hand and looks me in the eye. "I'm sorry for your loss."

All at once I realize this is the first of hundreds of times I will hear those words in the next few weeks. I now have a loss that others are sorry for.

"What time was he called?" I want to know, and they look up at the clock: 9:10. The same time Aaron was born.

They tell us we can stay with Reuel as long as we want, but first they need to make the room more presentable. We move in slow motion to the waiting area, where our friends are gathered. We are stunned, all of us grasping for hugs and comfort and simply being with those who loved Reuel and each other. Soon the nurse tells us we can be with him, and we become a single-file procession to his bed.

Reuel is cleaned up, but the intubation tube is still in his mouth. We look at him, and there is silence. I am comfortable, but I wonder how many of those around me have ever been so newly on the scene of a death. One by one, these friends who are our chosen family begin to tell their own experience of a loved one dying, how meaning- ful it was for family to gather around, just like we're doing. Marci's friend shares a particular memory of Reuel when he listened to her and made her feel better. Cate shares how her family sang "Amazing Grace" around her grandmother's bed after she died, and then Carla begins the song. We all join her. We sing the old hymns and tradi- tional spirituals that were the playlist of Reuel's life. How fitting, *I* think, that music helped Reuel survive some tumultuous years, and now it's helping us survive his passing.

I tuck my cold hands under his arm. He is still warm. As my hands drain his warmth, I shift position until I find another warm spot. I soak up all that warmth and change spots again. This is the last time Reuel will ever warm my hands. Eventually, there is no warmth remaining. We sing his body cool.

25
Catching My Breath

Six Weeks After Reuel's Death

Finally, I have the house to myself for a day. Extended stays of family and friends were healing, but I crave some time to myself. In fact, I want to catch up on finances, now that I unthawed the online banking freeze. So much for thinking I could guess Reuel's passwords before I got locked out, but there's nothing quite like a death certificate to inspire cooperation among the banks' customer service people.

I situate myself at the desk with fresh coffee and determination to plow through the accounts. Just as I reach for a new book of checks, I discover the next packet is missing the first three checks. Huh? Nothing is recorded in the register. Odd, especially considering how meticulous Reuel was with finances. I start the search function in the online account to track down the missing checks. Nothing—not for three months, six months, or the last nine months. Finally, at one year prior, the three checks appear, all made out to the same payee. Who the heck is Bill? And why is he getting so much of our money? And how could I not know about this?

Something clicks. I bolt down the stairs to the little cabinet, still positioned next to Reuel's recliner, still displaying the stained glass lamp his friend made. My mind floods with images and my body floods with adrenaline as I recall that Valentine's night three months ago when Reuel, tortured with pain, went to the hospital for the last time. My heart pounds as the scene plays out in my mind: just as we were to make our way to the car, he reached into his pocket, tucked something into the drawer of that cabinet, and then groaned with pain. His anguish was so distracting right then that I didn't ask about it. The few times it crossed my mind in the ensuing five weeks, I relegated it to a low spot on the priority list and decided to wait until he was back home so he could retrieve it himself.

Then he died.

Grief consumed me, still consumes and continues to munch holes in my memory.

Now, as I stand before that cabinet, my breathing ragged, I wonder how long Reuel held that object in his pocket. Did he retrieve it earlier that day? How could he? He could barely walk. Was it a gift for Valentine's Day? All I know is that this object is somehow connected to the three missing checks.

The house is perfectly quiet. I pull open the drawer, pick up what looks like a ring box, and gently open it. My eyes pop, my breath catches, my hand flies to my mouth. A diamond ring glints up at me, unlike any ring I've seen or would pick for myself. It is beautiful. I slam the lid shut, exhale. Too much. I feel warmth rush through me. I open the lid again, feel tears welling. I close the lid again as the tears begin to build. I collapse into the nearest chair as the gusher erupts.

How sweet the relief to sob in an empty house as the

memories play out. Six weeks ago, the last words he said before he died were about the ring. A few months ago, at Christmas, I opened the gift of diamond earrings while Reuel told me it was only part one. A year ago, when Reuel asked what I wanted for our thirty-fifth anniversary, I said "Bling!"

"He outdid himself with bling," I blubber into the quiet room.

A year ago! My mind flashes back to our discussion about retirement and savings.

"Babe, why don't I start depositing my private practice income into our other money-market account? That way, we can build some cash reserves," he said.

"Great!" I had encouraged. Then it hits me so hard my sobs stop. How sneaky of him! He had made a practice of showing me his deposits, describing how our account was accumulating. We even congratulated each other on what good savers we were. Meanwhile, I now grasp, he turned his deposits around and sent checks to this Bill guy.

Suddenly, Reuel is here in the room with me. In my mind, I see him sporting one of his Cheshire cat grins, his eyes barely containing his glee, his presence unmistakable. Delighted, he is teasing me. "See? When you thought I was so magnanimous, I was squirreling my money away for your new diamond. And you didn't suspect a thing! I couldn't wait to share this with you."

I start to chuckle, even though my cheeks are still damp. Soon I am hooting, or whatever the opposite of sobbing is. Reuel is laughing also. I look at the three "missing" checks again, and see that sure enough, he transacted this business a month or so before he was diagnosed. I laugh harder. We laugh together. This time tears roll because I am laughing so hard. Reuel's joy is contagious.

We spend the day together, his presence sometimes breathtakingly intense, other times a mere suggestion. Throughout the day, whenever I think about Reuel's ruse, I snicker. I don't want this day to end.

A few hours later, as I am filing a document from the hospital, I find two pieces of paper. One is a receipt from the mysterious "Bill" with an address several states away. It acknowledges the diamond earrings. Good, there's some closure for me that Bill is real with a real address.

The other paper is a letter Reuel wrote several years earlier, before our first cruise. It is addressed to our kids, just in case we didn't return from our trip. He wrote to them collectively, then had a paragraph exclusively for each. As I read, Reuel's presence returns to the room with me. Then, I don't know if he tells me or I think it myself, I understand that I will copy this letter to each child, with their specific messages, to give them on Reuel's birthday next week. After their individual paragraphs, he had written about his wishes for a memorial service.

Oh, why didn't we know about this six weeks ago? I hold my breath as I read:

Don't worry about what I would want, because by then, I won't care. Instead, do what is comforting to you. Open a good bottle of Bordeaux, and drink a toast to me.

Incredibly, we had successfully (if unknowingly) honored his wishes. I feel full with this knowledge and want to pause from reading in order to digest this richness.

Later, after drinking in the beauty of the day, I return to

read the last few paragraphs of his letter. He writes that it just occurred to him that I might survive him, and he assures me of what I meant to him, even admits how I was right about deciding to move and build the house. (Is it wrong for me to feel so gratified?) And then, stunningly, he closes his letter with the goodbye that perhaps he would have said to us six weeks ago, if he had been able.

Well, I could go on and on and on, but I'd have to end sometime and somehow. Please know how much I have loved you all, the best way I possibly could. There are many things I would wish to have done differently, but having each one of you in my life, my family, and our love is not one of those things. I don't want to say it but I must. Good bye—I love you forever—and in just another moment or two we will once again know each other but in a far more wonderful and limitless way.

Love always,
The energy formerly known as Reuel

Epilogue

"[T]he bad news is that you never completely get over the loss of your beloved. But this is also the good news. They live forever in your broken heart that doesn't seal back up. And you come through. It's like having a broken leg that never heals perfectly— that still hurts when the weather gets cold, but you learn to dance with the limp."
—Anne Lamott

Six Years Later

"Sweetheart, let's go ride our bikes."

"Just a minute. I've almost finished rewriting this chapter."

Reworking the chapter poked at old, tender wounds. Funny how my body remembers the pain of gutting through another piece of marital conflict, how my stomach braces as I recall jabbing Reuel about his rigid stance. And how, even now, my shoulders slump at the memory of how sluggish I was to confront myself: my impatience, my not-so-disguised criticism, and my unrealistic expectations. Ouch. Nothing about those hurtful memories feels like intimacy. I wonder again how our wounds weren't maritally mortal. I know we worked to keep a connection, but that kind of work is so demanding and requires such full engagement by both partners that I understand why many couples opt out of their marriages.

After I finally quit the keyboard, my mood casts a pall over our bike ride. I'm quiet as my legs pump, my thoughts circling like the wheels. Intimate relationships inevitably create pain. Am I up for it . . . again? Are the pain and work worth it . . . again? My thoughts continue cycling. Intimacy requires such hard, uphill efforts, I pant as I pedal faster toward the crest. But then, as the bike begins coasting, there's the exhilaration of those downhill speeds! Is the effort of the climb worth my shaky legs and sore quads tomorrow? I could save myself some work by avoiding any future bike rides and intimate relationships. Then again, I know what happens to my body if I don't work it, and I know what happens to my spirit if I avoid the kind of self-confrontation that intimacy demands.

After we get back to the house, I go to Peter, take a deep breath, and tell him what I've been thinking. He listens in that head-tilted way I've come to love, then exclaims, "Oh, sweetheart!" He enfolds me.

He is a different fit from Reuel, yet absolutely satisfying. Plus, he calls me "Sweetheart." I feel peace and warmth sweep through me.

Later that evening, it dawns on me that I unconsciously extended Peter an invitation to intimacy by revealing my old wounds and questions about whether I'm once again ready for the challenge of intimacy. By his careful listening, he accepts my invitation, and then extends one of his own by offering to hold me. Thus, the mystery of intimacy plays out: I once again risk being known, he accepts me and risks a vulnerable response, and the old pain from earlier in the day transforms into a loving tenderness.

I look over at Peter, now working on his laptop. Here is a man who crossed my path six years after Reuel left us, a man I've discovered is also willing to accept and extend invitations to intimacy by baring his soul and being known. My heart fills with love.

Yes, I decide again, *the hard work is worth it.*

Notes

Introduction
Definition of intimacy: Balswick, J.O. & Balswick, J. K. (2006). *A model for marriage.* Downers Grove, IL: Inter-Varsity Press.

Chapter 2: Co-Constructing
Opening quote: Real, T. (2018). *Fierce intimacy.* Sounds True, Unabridged edition, audio CD.

Chapter 3: Diving Presence and Dissonance
Opening quote: Lamott, A. (2000). *Traveling mercies: Some thoughts on faith* (p. 113). Palatine, IL: Anchor.

Chapter 4: Anxiety
Opening quote: Lerner, H. (2019, July 7). Why I love anxiety, and you should too. *Psychology Today.* Retrieved from https://www.psychologytoday.com/us/blog/the-dance-connection/201907/why-i-love-anxiety-and-you-should-too.

Chapter 5: Truths

Opening quote: Wakefield, C. (2021, p. 76). *The labyrinth of love: The path to a soulful relationship.*, Asheville, NC: Chiron.

Chapter 6: Trust

Opening quote: Perel, E. & Miller, M.A., Want to build trust in your relationship? Take risks. Retrieved from https://www.estherperel.com/blog/want-to-build-trust-in-your-relationship-take-risks.

Inside Look counseling session: Gottman, J.M. & Silver, N. (1999). *The seven principles for making marriage work.* New York: Crown Publishers.

Chapter 7: Doubt

Opening quote: Gay, R. (2017, p. 181). *Hunger: A memoir of (my) body.* London: Corsair.

Chapter 8: Connecting

Opening quote: Doherty, W. J. (2013, p. 156). *Take back your marriage: Sticking together in a world that pulls us apart.* New York: Guilford Press.

Inside Look teaching: Schnarch, D. (2009). *Passionate marriage: Keeping love and intimacy alive in committed relationships.* New York: Norton & Company.

Chapter 9: Yielding

Opening quote: Finkel, E. (2017, p. 97). *The all-or-nothing marriage: How the best marriages work.* New York: Dutton.

Reference to my mentor: Maddock, James W. Professor Emeritus, University of Minnesota, and Founder, Program in Human Sexuality, University of Minnesota Medical School.

Chapter 10: Bonds
Opening quote: Wakefield, C. (2021). (p. 22).

Chapter 11: Christmas
Opening quote: Butler-Robinson, C. (2021, July 8). Facebook posting, used by permission from Butler-Robinson, author of *The mud & the lotus: A guide and workbook for students of yoga.*

Reference to cancer like the presidency: Obama, M. (2012, Sept 4). Speech at the Democratic National Convention, Charlotte, NC. Retrieved from https://www.huffpost.com/entry/michelle-obama-speech_n_1856175.

Chapter 12: Standing Firm
Opening quote: Schnarch, D. (2009, pp. 105, 107). *Intimacy & desire.* NY: Beaufort Books.

Reference to spousal consent for medical treatment: retrieved from https://biotech.law.lsu.edu/Books/aspen/Aspen-Spouses.html.

Chapter 13: Letting Go

Opening quote: Angelou, M. Retrieved from https://everydaypower.com/maya-angelou-quotes/

Chapter 15: Hearts

Opening quote: Lerner, H. (2017, p. 12). *Why won't you apologize? Healing big betrayals and everyday hurts.* NY: Gallery Books.

Chapter 16: Who *IS* This?

Opening quote: Maddock, J.W. From "Jim-isms" booklet, 2005 at his retirement.

Chapter 17: Relief

Opening quote: Sams, J. & Carson, D. (1999, p. 21). *Medicine cards.* New York: St. Martin's Press.

Chapter 18: Trust Again

Opening quote: Wakefield, C. (2021). (p. 252).

Chapter 19: Balancing Between

Opening quote: Menakem, R. (2015, p. 79). *Rock the Boat: How to use conflict to heal and deepen your relationship.* Center City, MN: Hazelden Publishing.

Chapter 21: Crossroads

Opening quote: Finkel, E. J. (2017). Cited by E. Perel. Retrieved from https://www.estherperel.com/blog/want-to-build-trust-in-your-relationship-take-risks.

Chapter 23: It's Enough

Opening quote: Brown, B. (2015, p. 182). *Rising Strong: How the Ability to Reset Transforms the Way We Live, Love, Parent, and Lead*. NY: Random House.

Chapter 24: Transformation

Opening quote: Finley, J. (2018, October 23) Traumatization of spirituality. Daily Meditations, Center for Action and Contemplation. Retrieved from https://cac.org/traumatization-of-spirituality-2018-10-23/www.cac.org.

Epilogue

Opening quote: Lamott, A. Retrieved from https://www.azquotes.com/quote/362774

Acknowledgments

Relationships come in all forms, including my relationship with this book. During the process of writing I was at various times infatuated with it, furious, exhausted, enamored, estranged, and eventually at peace with it. Just as close friends, mentors, and the occasional counselor help us navigate relationships, I've had many resources to further this book.

Cindy Barrilleaux was an early guide, helping me channel my raw grief into a story, then multiple stories. She was part therapist, part writing coach, and part spiritual director who challenged me to dig deeper for truth. I'm sure my grief and my writing would have looked very different without her coaching.

Writing groups over the years kept the relationship with my book alive. Thanks to Maria, Teresa, Janet, Mary, Gwen, Laurel, Brier, Ginny. I'm grateful to those who read early drafts and offered feedback, including Rebekah Jensen, Lisa Jensen, Aneta Stevenson, Scott Edelstein, Peter Jensen, and Marci Tiesel. The timing of Elizabeth Shores' encouraging comments helped push the manuscript to the next phase.

The process of therapy and teaching are mutually influential. I've been a client, a student, a therapist, and a teacher, all experiences which ripple in their impact through me and back into my relationships, including that with my book. I'm thankful for the influences of these colleagues and friends: Noel Larson, Bill Doherty, the late James Maddock, Carla Dahl, Gail Hartman, Cate Lally, Brier Miller, Resmaa Menakem, Laurel Jung, Lori Carter, Charme Davidson, and Belle Yaffe.

I hold the deepest gratitude and respect for those clients who invited me into their courageous journeys of healing. Your work also continues to ripple in its impact within me and beyond.

A huge resource continues to be Erin Wood, publisher and editor extraordinaire, who made this publishing process fun by sharing laughs, tears, and inspiration. You have an uncanny knack for knowing when to confront and when to hold my hand. Your style of editing teaches me to be a better writer. Thanks also to Gabrielle Thurman and Emma Lassiter for their sharp eyes and finishing polish, and to Amy Ashford's creative services.

My relationship to the book closely parallels my relationship to Reuel, whom I recognize for providing such a rich source of data about intimacy, for inviting me to my best self, and for loving me so completely. You always believed I would write a book. I thought we would do it together, and, well, I guess we did.

Finally, I am grateful to Peter for falling in love with the story of Reuel and Judy. Thank you for persistent challenges about what I really wanted to say, for encouraging me, for falling in love with me—not just the story—and for being the kind of person whose invitation to intimacy I wanted to accept.

About The Author

JUDY TIESEL-JENSEN has been a therapist for over thirty years. She is a Licensed Marriage & Family Therapist and Psychologist Emeritus and holds professional memberships in the American Association of Marriage & Family Therapists (AAMFT) and EMDRIA (Eye Movement Desensitization & Reprocessing International Association). She was among the first to get advanced training in Discernment Counseling.

Judy pursued a Ph.D. in Marriage and Family Therapy to fulfill her long-held interest in couple relationships. From early in her first marriage, she and her late husband—also a licensed counselor—led parenting workshops and marriage enrichment retreats, and eventually saw couples together in counseling. Her private practice in the Minneapolis-St. Paul area specialized in couple therapy and trauma. She taught marriage and family therapy students for over twenty years, was lead researcher for the Minnesota Family Strengths Project, and has served on boards locally and nationally for family organizations.

Judy is now creatively retired and lives in Arkansas with her husband, Peter. Together they have eight children and fifteen grandchildren. She enjoys living on the river and watching pelicans from her writing desk.